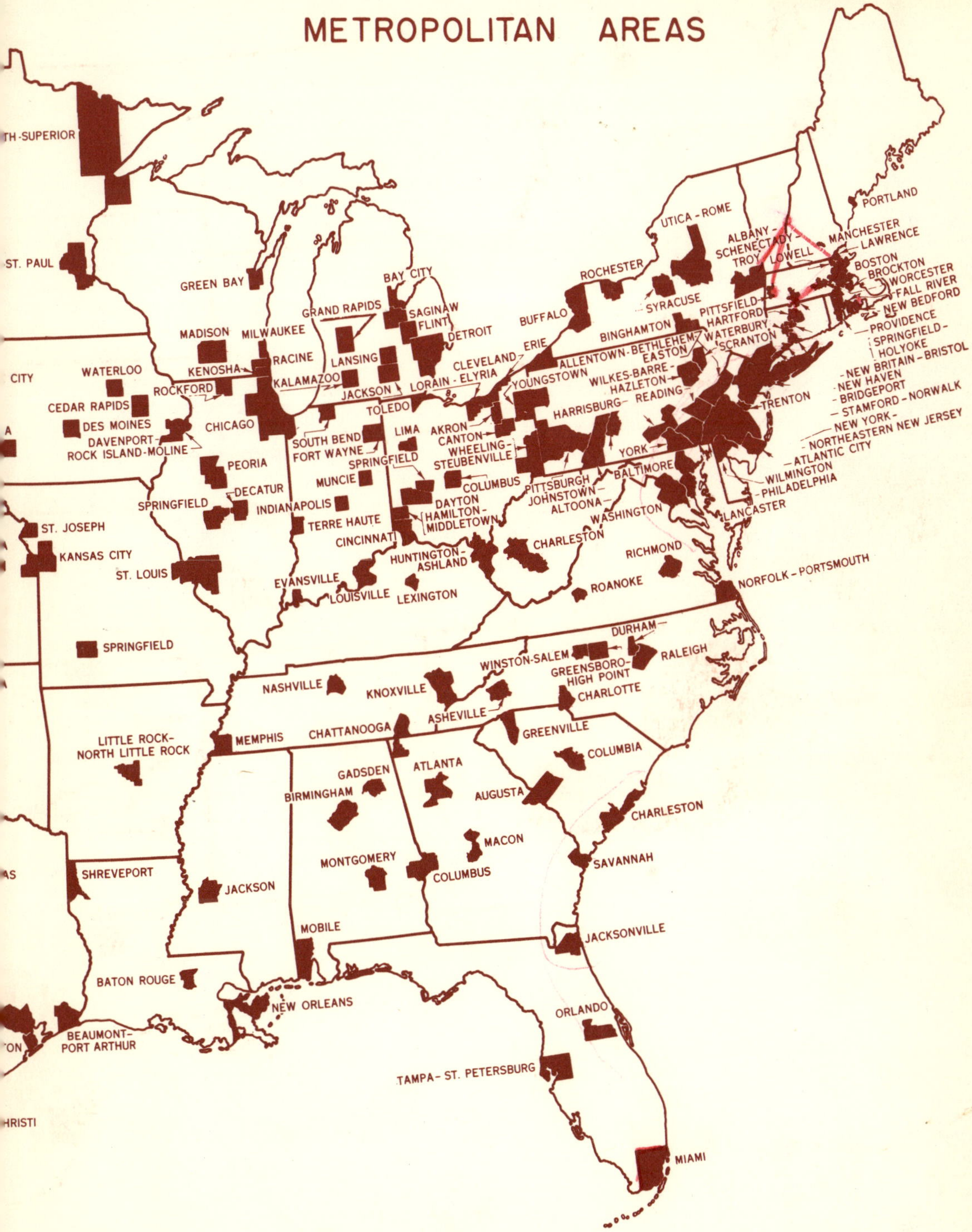

*Dartmouth College
Library*
purchased this book
from the income of
the fund established
in memory of
E. PHELPS JOHNSON
of the class of 1912

THE STATES
and the
METROPOLITAN PROBLEM

THE STATES
and the
METROPOLITAN PROBLEM

*A REPORT TO THE
GOVERNORS' CONFERENCE*

The Council of State Governments
1313 East 60th Street
Chicago 37, Illinois

COPYRIGHT, 1956, BY
THE COUNCIL OF STATE GOVERNMENTS
1313 EAST SIXTIETH STREET
CHICAGO 37, ILLINOIS

Library of Congress Catalog Card Number: 56-10396

PRINTED IN THE UNITED STATES OF AMERICA

A Study of
The Problem of Government
in Metropolitan Areas

JOHN C. BOLLENS
Director of the Study

FOREWORD

The Governors' Conference, by a resolution adopted at its 1955 annual meeting, directed the Council of State Governments to study the problem of government in metropolitan areas. To make this study, the Council was fortunate in obtaining the services of John C. Bollens of the Department of Political Science, University of California, Los Angeles.

Briefly stated, the problem of government in metropolitan areas arises from the division of power and responsibility among a host of separate local governmental units. None of them currently is able to provide a sufficient number of services and facilities on an area-wide basis, and so none is able to meet effectively the needs and problems which are of an area-wide nature.

This report reviews the experience with six major devices by which citizens have attempted to alter governmental patterns to solve the problem. It appraises each of these methods and suggests the extent to which each is useful.

Throughout the study, attention is given to means by which the states have attempted to resolve the difficulties confronting metropolitan areas. No single panacea is suggested, but three approaches to the metropolitan problem—federation, the urban county, and the metropolitan special district—are recommended as offering the greatest promise in most areas. The final section of the report stresses several responsibilities that seem advisable for the states to assume in working cooperatively with local governments and organizations toward an adequate solution of the metropolitan problem.

Numerous organizations and agencies, public and private, in all sections of the country have been concerned with and are working on this difficult subject. Many of them have given us the benefit of their advice and counsel in developing this report. We are most grateful to them.

Our hope is that the study will be valuable to Governors, state legislators, local officials and other groups and individuals in their consideration of one of the most acute and challenging problems facing an increasingly urban America.

FRANK BANE
Executive Director

CONTENTS

Part One. Metropolitan Areas: The Setting and The Problem

Defining Metropolitan Areas 3

The Rise of Metropolitan Areas: Some Contributing Factors 5

Characteristics of Metropolitan Areas 7

The Metropolitan Problem: A Series of Problems 17

Part Two. The Metropolitan Record: Approaches to Solving the Problem

1. Annexation 25
   - The Nature of Early Annexation 25
   - The Decline of Annexation 27
   - The Post World War II Revival 28
   - Need for Changes in Annexation Laws 33
   - Annexation in Texas 35
   - Annexation in Virginia 40
   - Implementation of the Laws 49

2. City-County Consolidation 53
   - The New Orleans Consolidation 53
   - The Boston Consolidation 54
   - The Philadelphia Consolidation 57
   - The New York Consolidation 61
   - The Baton Rouge Consolidation 65
   - General Conclusions about Completed Consolidations 68
   - Rejected Consolidation Proposals 71
   - City-County Consolidation: An Appraisal 74

3. City-County Separation 76
   - Comparison of Four City-County Separations 76
   - City-County Separation in Virginia 81

Negligible Recent Interest 83
City-County Separation: An Appraisal 84

4. Federation (The Borough Plan) 86
Attempts at Federation 86
Federation in Action: The Toronto Area 96
Federation: An Appraisal 103

5. Functional Transfers and Joint Efforts 105
Major Characteristics 105
The Urban or Metropolitan County Movement 106
The Urban County Development in California 111
An Urban County Reversal 113
Functional Transfers and Joint Efforts: An Appraisal 114

6. Metropolitan Special Districts 117
Reasons for Growth 117
Principal Characteristics 119
Metropolitan Special Districts: An Appraisal 121

PART THREE. THE RESPONSIBILITIES OF THE STATES

A Suggested Program for the States 128
Recent Growth of Interest 130
Authorizing General Metropolitan Units 132
Appraising Local Governments 140
A Research and Service Agency 144
A Continuing Responsibility for the States 147

INDEX 149

Part One

METROPOLITAN AREAS:
THE SETTING AND THE PROBLEM

PART ONE

Metropolitan Areas: The Setting and the Problem

Defining Metropolitan Areas

THE rise of metropolitan areas has become one of the most significant and spectacular population trends in the United States, and it has led to a major, largely unsolved problem of government.

Each metropolitan area occupies densely settled territory, the central and other portions of which possess important economic and social relationships. The various definitions of "metropolitan area" generally include these elements but they often disagree over the territorial extent of the area involved. Such disagreement is inevitable, since individuals and organizations apply a variety of criteria, singly or in combination, in trying to determine metropolitan boundaries. Some of the indices that have been utilized are population total or density, newspaper circulation areas, transportation facilities and rates, tax reports, postal receipts, and wealth and consumption levels. Others include market characteristics, retail sales, wholesale activities, industrial distribution, manufacturing pattern, leisure-time facilities, and uses of automobiles and communication media.

The Most Widely Used Definition

The definition of metropolitan areas currently in most general use was first applied by the United States Bureau of the Census in 1950. It had been worked out under the direction of the Bureau of the Budget by the Federal Committee on Standard Metropolitan Areas, consisting of representatives from a number of national government agencies. Each "standard metropolitan area" as identified by the Census Bureau now consists, in general, of at least one central city of not less than 50,000 population and the entire county in which it is located. In addition, it includes other entire counties that are contiguous to the first county, are primarily places of employment or residence for concentrations of non-agricultural workers, and possess extensive economic and social contacts with the central county. Each city of at least 50,000 people is, therefore, in a standard metropolitan area, and two or more cities of such minimum population within twenty miles of each other are usually in the same standard metropolitan area.

Only in New England are metropolitan areas not defined by the Census Bureau in terms of whole counties. Because the town instead of the county is utilized by the bureau as the primary unit for reporting purposes in this region, metropolitan areas in New England are based on contiguous towns and cities of certain population densities. These governmental units ordinarily must contain at least 150 people per square mile or, where strong economic and social integration is evident, at least 100 people per square mile.[1]

The definition prepared for the 1950 census is the latest in a series employed by the Census Bureau. Each of them has been widely used. The bureau originally recognized the existence of metropolitan areas in 1886, in its *Report on Social Statistics*, and it formulated its first definition of them for the decennial census of 1910. The difficulty of deciding upon the indices to be applied in determining the territorial limits involved is well illustrated by the Census Bureau's experience. Various factors initially included by it, such as a standard of population density for territory adjacent to a central city, or a rule on maximum distance of such territory from the central city, were subsequently altered and later eliminated. In preparing for the 1930 census the bureau, in cooperation with the United States Chamber of Commerce, attempted to utilize criteria of commercial, social and economic activity, but it abandoned the effort because the data lacked sufficient uniformity. Despite the various alterations adopted, however, the Census Bureau has been consistent in adhering to the concept of a central city of a specific minimum population as a basic element in its definitions.

Although providing simply an approximation of the actual limits of each metropolitan area, the bureau's definition of 1950 is more valuable than its earlier ones. It increases the comparability of data collected by various national government agencies by furnishing a standard that can be used by all of them. It fits better than previous norms into the general

---

[1] For a discussion of a number of indices employed by private organizations and public agencies such as the Census Bureau, see National Resources Committee, *Population Statistics 3. Urban Data* (Washington: 1937), pp. 32–36; Warren S. Thompson, *The Growth of Metropolitan Districts in the United States: 1900–1940* (Washington: U.S. Bureau of the Census, 1947); and U.S. Bureau of the Census, *1950 Census of Population*, Volume 1 (Washington: 1952).

system of Census Bureau definitions and concepts. It is generally more adequate for research workers and administrators concerned with metropolitan developments in labor markets, transportation, housing, marketing, and population growth and distribution.[2] It more accurately indicates the recent territorial growth of metropolitan areas.

The new definition is receiving wide utilization because the several divisions of the Census Bureau constitute the principal agencies that collect metropolitan data on a nation-wide scale. Other public and private organizations that gather data frequently use Census Bureau definitions to make their findings comparable.

Despite its usefulness for comparisons and generalizations, the 1950 definition is mainly a broad working concept.[3] It is therefore subject to modifications growing out of determinations made by public officials and private citizens in individual states and metropolitan areas. For example, governmental reorganization proposals in some metropolitan areas may justifiably be applied to a smaller or a larger amount of territory than that delineated by the definition. Regardless of the definition used, however, there is growing recognition of the existence, implications and approximate boundaries of metropolitan areas.

The Rise of Metropolitan Areas: Some Contributing Factors

The extensive development of metropolitan areas results from many factors. Agricultural improvements forced many former farm workers to go to urban locations to earn a livelihood. The development of power-machine industry, especially in the form of electrical energy which could be transmitted and applied long distances from its source, made possible a wider distribution of people, industry and commerce. Continued advances in medicine and sanitation substantially lowered the death rate. All of these factors facilitated the metropolitan movement, but the immediate causes that brought on the highly intensified growth of metropolitan areas were in the field of transportation. Widespread use of the internal combustion engine, the establishment of modern

[2] The first three advantages are discussed in Donald J. Bogue, *Population Growth in Standard Metropolitan Areas, 1900–1950* (Washington: Housing and Home Finance Agency, 1953), pp. 3–4.

[3] In general, metropolitan areas as discussed in this study are identical with "standard metropolitan areas" defined for the 1950 census.

roads, and improvements in rapid mass transit all were basic. Private automobiles, in particular, provided increased flexibility and individuality in transportation. Together with truck transport and high-speed interurban trains, they greatly increased the freedom of movement of people and goods over a widening area, whose parts thus became increasingly interrelated.

Technological changes had to be supported by human wishes to make large-scale metropolitan development a reality. In many instances, although people wanted to be near the central city for work and social opportunities, they established their homes outside its limits in the hope of acquiring more pleasant living conditions. New or improved transportation facilities gave city dwellers the opportunity to move from the city, upon which they continued to have various types of economic or social dependence. Similar opportunities were available to business and other organizations. Thus, numerous people, industries, manufacturing plants and trade establishments settled in the outlying sections. Some relocated from sites within the city, and others transferred from locations outside of the metropolitan area.

New communities developed, and new governments were created to provide services and regulation. The relatively detached economic and social position of older, established cities situated within ten to twenty miles of the central city disappeared. The comparative self-sufficiency of many urban localities gave way to greater interdependence in a metropolitan area. Numerous old and new settlements alike therefore became interacting parts of a metropolitan whole, and a heavy volume of travel and contact, both for work and social purposes, became common between the central city and other sections.

The factors that have permitted and expedited the development of metropolitan areas are still present and active. Some have had appreciably stronger effect in recent years than before. Widespread use of private automobiles and continued improvements in roads are examples. No major counter factor, such as dispersion to lessen the potential effects of atomic war, has yet taken hold. Consequently there are no current indications that the metropolitan trend—already of enormous proportions—has reached its peak. Obviously, therefore, the problems resulting from the rise and expansion of metropolitan areas will not be solved merely by passage of time. Instead, the difficulties must be expected to become more aggravated unless remedial actions are taken.

The existence of metropolitan areas in the United States is no recent

The Setting and the Problem

innovation. Those of which Philadelphia, New York and Boston are the focal points materialized in their first stages in the late eighteenth and early nineteenth centuries. It has been in the present century, however, that metropolitan areas have increased most impressively in number, population and territorial extent, and also in their significance to the nation as a whole.

Characteristics of Metropolitan Areas

A General Development

Metropolitan areas are large in total number and they represent a nation-wide rather than a regional development. There are 172 such areas in the continental United States, comprising territory in forty-two

TABLE 1

GEOGRAPHICAL LOCATION OF METROPOLITAN AREAS BY STATES

State	Number of metropolitan areas entirely or partly within the state*	State	Number of metropolitan areas entirely or partly within the state*
Alabama	5	Nebraska	2
Arizona	2	Nevada	0
Arkansas	2	New Hampshire	1
California	8	New Jersey	6
Colorado	2	New Mexico	1
Connecticut	7	New York	7
Delaware	1	North Carolina	6
District of Columbia	1	North Dakota	0
Florida	4	Ohio	14
Georgia	6	Oklahoma	2
Idaho	0	Oregon	1
Illinois	7	Pennsylvania	13
Indiana	8	Rhode Island	2
Iowa	7	South Carolina	4
Kansas	3	South Dakota	1
Kentucky	5	Tennessee	3
Louisiana	3	Texas	15
Maine	1	Utah	2
Maryland	2	Vermont	0
Massachusetts	10	Virginia	5
Michigan	8	Washington	4
Minnesota	2	West Virginia	3
Mississippi	1	Wisconsin	6
Missouri	4	Wyoming	0
Montana	0		

* The total exceeds 172 because some metropolitan areas are interstate and are counted for each state involved.

states and in the District of Columbia.[4] The only states that do not currently contain at least part of an area defined by the Census Bureau as metropolitan are Idaho, Montana, Nevada, North Dakota, Vermont and Wyoming, and in some of them certain sections are approaching this status. Metropolitan areas thus are found in the great majority of geographical regions of the United States. The overwhelming proportion of the states have experienced their development in from one to fifteen urban sections. (See Table 1.) Consequently, the metropolitan trend has much current influence in important portions of most states and affects many people in individual states. Justifiably it is a matter of increasing and general state concern.

Rapid, Sustained Population Growth

More than half of the nation's population lives in metropolitan areas. In 1950 the number was approximately 84 million, or 56 per cent of the national total. There were fourteen metropolitan areas of more than 1,000,000 each, nineteen of 500,000–1,000,000, fifty-seven of 200,000–500,000, sixty-one of 100,000–200,000, and seventeen of 50,000–100,000.[5] This means that more than seven-tenths of all metropolitan areas had between 100,000 and 500,000 inhabitants. However, slightly more than one-half of the metropolitan population resided in the fourteen largest metropolitan areas. In the same year 64 per cent of the people of the United States were located in urban territory. In other words, almost nine of every ten individuals living in urban areas were inhabitants of metropolitan areas. Thus, in substantial part, the long-time urban trend has become a metropolitan trend.

Rapid increases in population have been occurring in metropolitan areas in general. During the entire current century the metropolitan population has been growing faster than the national population. The differential between the two narrowed during the 1930's but became particularly evident again in the following ten years. From 1940 to 1950

[4] The metropolitan area definition first applied by the Census Bureau in 1950 is used throughout this consideration of various characteristics. The data on number and territory include four additional metropolitan areas recognized since the *1950 Census of Population* and three that have been enlarged territorially since then. Much of the subsequent discussion of population and governmental units is necessarily based on the complete Census Bureau tabulations for the 168 metropolitan areas determined in 1950.

[5] If the four newly recognized metropolitan areas are included and the three redefined ones are substituted, the totals are altered in three population classes: fifty-eight of 200,000–500,000, sixty-two of 100,000–200,000, and nineteen of 50,000–100,000.

The Setting and the Problem

the country's population growth took place largely in metropolitan areas. While the number of people elsewhere increased by slightly more than 6 per cent, the metropolitan population grew by 22 per cent and accounted for more than four-fifths of the national gain in the decade. This much greater proportionate growth was attributable principally to migrations from non-metropolitan sectors, although the rising metropolitan birth rate was a factor.

The growth of the metropolitan population, however, did not proceed during the decade at an approximately even rate in all areas. A few actually lost population, and several gained less than the national percentage increase outside of metropolitan areas. On the other hand, about one-fifth grew by more than 40 per cent over their 1940 totals; significantly, they were found in each of the major population classes of metropolitan areas. The highest proportion of metropolitan areas making gains of more than 40 per cent was in the medium-sized population class of 200,000 to 500,000; approximately one-fourth in this category had such increases.

Among the various classes containing less than 1,000,000 people each, very high percentage growths were registered from 1940 to 1950 by the metropolitan areas whose central cities are Albuquerque, New Mexico (an increase of 109 per cent); Lubbock, Texas (95 per cent); San Diego, California (92 per cent); Miami, Florida (85 per cent); and Phoenix, Arizona (78 per cent). In the group with more than 1,000,000 population each, impressive percentage increases were recorded by the metropolitan areas of which the central cities are San Francisco-Oakland, California (53 per cent); Washington, D.C. (51 per cent); and Los Angeles, California (50 per cent). Gains of smaller proportions were the trend in most other metropolitan areas regardless of their size.

Extensive Suburban Growth

The main increase in metropolitan population has been taking place outside the central cities. This has been a steady trend during most of the century. Present in most metropolitan areas by the 1930's, it was particularly apparent in the decade from 1940 to 1950. In these ten years the number of people in central cities increased by approximately 14 per cent, a gain largely attributable to an excess of births over deaths and virtually the same as that of the national population as a whole. Meanwhile, the total in the other portions of metropolitan areas grew by more than 35 per cent. The outlying portions accounted for more than three-fifths of the metropolitan growth and nearly one-half of the national population increase. Less than a fifth of the central cities grew faster than the other sections of metropolitan areas.

Within the metropolitan trend a large-scale decentralization has materialized. Consequently, approximately one-fourth of the central cities do not contain a majority of the people of the metropolitan areas in which they are located. Such population distribution is present in at least one metropolitan area in each of nineteen states and exists in most metropolitan sectors of California and Pennsylvania. Numerous new metropolitan residents have settled in the outlying portions, and some people have moved to them from the central cities. Increasing numbers of people are residing in incorporated and unincorporated localities that are beyond the service and regulatory jurisdictions of the central cities.

The Spread of Metropolitan Population

The territorial size of metropolitan areas has been enlarging, and now totals 7 per cent of all territory within the states. Particularly since the 1930's the spread of population over a wider area has been supplanting the previous relative compactness of metropolitan growth. The 1950 Census Bureau definition, which generally determined larger sizes for metropolitan areas, was in part a recognition of this fact. Population growth has extended beyond the metropolitan boundaries determined in earlier definitions. Between 1940 and 1950, for example, there was a very rapid population increase in the territory outside of the earlier defined limits but within the boundaries now established in the 1950 definition. Moreover, in this period, the population gain at what are now the outer borders of the newly defined metropolitan area usually was more rapid than for the metropolitan area as a whole.[6]

Recent Continuation of Population Trends

Detailed data as to population trends since the 1950 census will not be established until the results of the next decennial census are available. However, a recent sample survey by the Census Bureau of civilian population furnishes estimates as of 1955 that apparently have consider-

[6] Bogue, *Population Growth in Standard Metropolitan Areas, 1900–1950*, pp. 17–18.

The Setting and the Problem

able reliability.[7] The survey reveals that several metropolitan population developments readily apparent from 1940 to 1950 not only have continued but have accelerated during the subsequent five years. Population growth has taken place largely in metropolitan areas. The portions of metropolitan areas outside central cities have increased much more rapidly than central cities. The proportion of people residing at the outer borders of metropolitan areas has grown faster than the population of metropolitan areas as a whole.

TABLE 2

ESTIMATED CIVILIAN POPULATION OF THE UNITED STATES BY METROPOLITAN AREAS AND NON-METROPOLITAN TERRITORY: APRIL, 1955

Residence	Number of people	Per cent increase 1950 to 1955
Total	161,461,000	7.9
Metropolitan areas	95,304,000	13.7
Central cities	51,023,000	3.8
Outside central cities	44,281,000	27.8
Urban	28,236,000	19.1
Rural	16,045,000	46.5
Other territory	66,157,000	0.5
Urban	24,217,000	5.0
Rural	41,940,000	−1.9

Source: United States Bureau of the Census, *Current Population Reports*, Series P-20, No. 63 (Washington: 1955), p. 1. The 168 metropolitan areas of 1950 were utilized in the classifications.

According to the sample survey, in the five-year period that ended in April, 1955, the increase in metropolitan areas was approximately 11,500,000 and that of the reminder of the country was only 300,000. With a total population of more than 95,000,000, metropolitan areas have 59 per cent of the population of the nation as compared to 56 per cent in 1950. The population in the portions of metropolitan areas outside central cities grew seven times as fast as that of the central cities. Approximately 46 per cent of all metropolitan residents now live in the non-central city sections. Moreover, the total number of people of the

[7] Military personnel, who were counted in the metropolitan area population totals in the *1950 Census of Population*, were excluded from the 1955 survey. The 1955 totals and the five-year comparisons in this section and in the following table are therefore based entirely on civilian population.

non-central city portions classified as rural by the Census Bureau in 1950, and located in large part at the outer borders of metropolitan areas, enlarged almost three and one-half times as fast as the entire metropolitan population. On the basis of the latest data, it thus is evident that the population growth of metropolitan areas and the decentralization of population within them are not slowing down but are proceeding at a very rapid pace.

Predominantly Intracounty

Most metropolitan areas—almost seven of every ten—contain the territory of a single county, but a significant number are intercounty.[8] Furthermore, many that are intercounty are also interstate. Of thirty metropolitan areas that are intercounty and entirely within one state, nineteen involve two counties. Consisting of three counties each are six metropolitan areas whose central cities are Albany-Schenectady-Troy, New York; Atlanta, Georgia; Brockton, Massachusetts; Detroit, Michigan; Knoxville, Tennessee; and New Orleans, Louisiana. Three metropolitan areas—Denver, Colorado; Minneapolis-St. Paul, Minnesota; and Pittsburgh, Pennsylvania—include four counties each.[9] One (Boston) involves five counties and another (San Francisco-Oakland) has six.

Metropolitan situations involving two or more counties in the same state are not exclusively a characteristic of the more populous areas. Although proportionately the largest population class (over 1,000,000) has the most metropolitan areas of this type, the medium category (200,000–500,000) presents a slightly higher percentage than does the group ranging from 500,000 to 1,000,000. There are only isolated examples in the two smallest categories, of 50,000 to 100,000 and 100,000 to 200,000.

The greatest significance of intercounty metropolitan areas, however, is not their size. Many of them are larger territorially than those within

[8] Consolidated or separated city-counties have been considered as counties only when the Census Bureau and the Federal Committee on Standard Metropolitan Areas have so classified them in determining metropolitan territory. The use of contiguous cities and towns in New England necessitates in some instances the inclusion of parts of counties rather than entire counties as in all other states. U.S. Office of the President, Bureau of the Budget, *Standard Metropolitan Area Definitions* (Washington: 1954).

[9] With one exception (New York–Northeastern New Jersey), metropolitan areas are identified by the names of all of their central cities, although numerous other governments exist within them.

The Setting and the Problem

a single county, but this is not universally the case; areas of counties vary considerably on a state-by-state basis and in some instances appreciably within a single state. The real importance of the intercounty status is that the metropolitan territory is not within the limits of any one general unit of local government. This is a matter that requires close consideration in the formulation of metropolitan reorganization proposals.

Interstate Metropolitan Areas

The territory of twenty-four metropolitan areas is interstate. Such sectors are most usual in the two largest population classes, but again, medium-sized metropolitan areas have considerable representation. Only a few interstate metropolitan areas are in the two smallest population groups. Twenty-six states and the District of Columbia have territory in one or more interstate metropolitan areas. A number of states have territory in several of them; for example, parts of Kentucky, New Jersey and Ohio are in four such areas, and portions of Georgia, Illinois, Indiana, Massachusetts and Pennsylvania are in three. Table 3 indicates the diversity that interstate metropolitan areas exhibit as to population and as to number of states and counties involved.

Metropolitan areas in general represent a concern of many state governments because a large proportion of the total state population resides in them and because they characteristically involve intergovernmental problems. Interstate metropolitan areas in particular need state-level attention. About two of every five metropolitan inhabitants live in interstate metropolitan areas, and certain activities in such areas require cooperation between at least two state governments. In addition to twenty-four interstate metropolitan areas, twenty-nine others currently border state lines. These twenty-nine contain approximately 12 per cent of the total metropolitan population of the country, and population trends indicate that some of them soon will become interstate. Thus the interstate problem seems about to become more extensive. More than a fourth of the nation's people reside in metropolitan areas that are either currently or potentially interstate.

Several areas present special territorial difficulties. One interstate metropolitan area of medium size—Huntington, West Virginia–Ashland, Kentucky—involves three states. Another, among the most populous in the nation (Washington, D.C.), concerns two states and the

District of Columbia. In these instances tri-state or two-state and national cooperation are necessary. Several metropolitan areas, including those whose central cities are Buffalo, Detroit and El Paso, although not interstate, are in fact international. Seven others—centering on Bay City, Chicago, Cleveland, Duluth-Superior, Erie, Milwaukee and Toledo—border on lakes that involve them in decisions of international importance on water supply and water pollution. Here state-national-international agreement is appropriate.

TABLE 3

INTERSTATE METROPOLITAN AREAS

Metropolitan area	1950 official population	States possessing part of territory*	Number of counties
Allentown-Bethlehem-Easton	437,824	Pa., N.J.	3
Augusta	162,013	Ga., S.C.	2
Chattanooga	246,453	Tenn., Ga.	2
Chicago	5,495,364	Ill., Ind.	6
Cincinnati	904,402	Ohio, Ky.	3
Columbus	170,541	Ga., Ala.	3
Davenport-Rock Island-Moline	234,256	Iowa, Ill.	2
Duluth-Superior	252,777	Minn., Wis.	2
Evansville	191,137	Ind., Ky.	2
Fall River	137,298	Mass., R.I.	2
Huntington-Ashland	245,795	W.Va., Ky., Ohio	4
Kansas City, Missouri	814,357	Mo., Kans.	4
Louisville	576,900	Ky., Ind.	3
New York–Northeastern New Jersey	12,911,994	N.Y., N.J.	17
Omaha	366,395	Neb., Iowa	3
Philadelphia	3,671,048	Pa., N.J.	8
Portland	704,829	Ore., Wash.	4
Providence	737,203	R.I., Mass.	6
St. Louis	1,681,281	Mo., Ill.	4
Springfield-Holyoke	407,255	Mass., Conn.	3
Washington	1,464,089	D.C., Md., Va.	4
Wheeling-Steubenville	354,092	W.Va., Ohio	6
Wilmington	268,387	Del., N.J.	2
Youngstown	528,498	Ohio, Pa.	3

* The state containing the central city (or the more populous one when there are two central cities) is listed first.

As metropolitan areas have grown in number, population and territory, the interest of state governments in them has grown. Increasingly, states are striving to determine their proper roles in metropolitan situations.

Governmental Complexity

The common pattern of governments functioning in metropolitan areas is complex and confusing. The number of local governmental

The Setting and the Problem 15

units is large, averaging ninety-six in each metropolitan area.[10] Moreover, several types of local governments are in operation, and they generally differ as to functions and the means of financing granted to them. The variations are still more pronounced in numerous interstate metropolitan areas. Comparable units, situated on opposite sides of a state boundary, operate under different state constitutions, different state laws and may differ in functional and financial authority. Usually metropolitan areas contain one or more classes of municipalities, one or more counties, and a variety of special districts.[11] In certain regions, towns or townships also are present. Many or all of these local governments individually occupy only portions of the metropolitan area.

As metropolitan areas have become more populous and extensive, local governments in them ordinarily have increased in number. This is apparent among incorporated places and is particularly noticeable among non-school special districts. The only numerical reduction in recent years has been that of school districts, and their decrease in metropolitan areas generally has been much less than in rural portions of some states.

The government of metropolitan areas, already complicated in the early decades of the century, has become more complex. Fourteen per cent of all local governments in the United States are located in metropolitan areas. For each 1,000 square miles in metropolitan areas there are slightly more than seventy-five local governments—more than double the number for 1,000 square miles of non-metropolitan territory.

Individually, the more populous metropolitan areas are generally the most complex governmentally. For example, the three largest contain the most governmental units and are interstate. The New York metropolitan area has 1,071 governmental units, the Chicago area 960, and the area centering on Philadelphia 702. There are important exceptions to this pattern, the most striking of which is the Madison, Wisconsin, metropolitan area. Ranking 102nd in population in 1950, it stood eleventh in number of local governmental units, with 292.

[10] Although the focus here is upon local governments, the national government and the state governments also have major effects on various metropolitan developments through field offices in numerous metropolitan areas and through programs carried out from the capitals.

[11] In some metropolitan areas, the central city completely or substantially surrounds one or more other cities. The Boston, Cincinnati, Los Angeles, Omaha, Pittsburgh and Tacoma metropolitan areas are examples.

In proportion to population the class of metropolitan areas with the least populous central cities have the most local governments.[12] In 1950 the five metropolitan areas with the most populous central cities had approximately 29,500,000 people and 3,386 local governments. The seventy-seven metropolitan areas with central cities of 50,000 to 100,000 inhabitants had about 40 per cent as much total population and almost 1,400 more local governmental units.

TABLE 4

NUMBER OF LOCAL GOVERNMENTS IN METROPOLITAN AREAS BY TYPE OF GOVERNMENT: 1952

SIZE OF LARGEST CITY IN EACH METROPOLITAN AREA	NUMBER OF METROPOLITAN AREAS	1950 POPULATION IN THOUSANDS	Total	Counties	Townships	Municipalities	School districts	Non-school special districts
Total.............	168	84,671	16,210	256	2,328	3,164	7,864	2,598
Over 1,000,000......	5	29,463	3,386	30	465	748	1,600	543
500,000–1,000,000...	13	18,246	2,628	37	346	694	1,125	426
250,000–500,000.....	18	9,854	1,800	32	108	364	853	443
100,000–250,000.....	55	15,487	3,613	66	728	606	1,563	650
50,000–100,000.....	77	11,621	4,783	91	681	752	2,723	536

Source: Adapted from U.S. Bureau of the Census, Governments Division, *Local Government in Metropolitan Areas*, State and Local Government Special Studies No. 36 (Washington: 1954), p. 7. The classifications are according to the population of the largest city in each metropolitan area and not by the total population of each metropolitan area.

Local governments in metropolitan areas present a bewildering pattern both because of their extreme numbers and their frequent territorial overlapping. Most of their boundaries are not coterminous with one another. In some states, for example, a city, a county, and a township occupy part of the same territory and therefore overlie portions of one another's jurisdiction. In many instances special districts increase the overlapping maze. Unlike other classes of governments, special districts may generally function in an area regardless of what other governments exist there. As a result, several types of special districts, of which school districts are simply one kind, occupy portions or all of the area of one another, as well as territory of other local governments.

[12] Coleman Woodbury, "Suburbanization and Suburbia," *American Journal of Public Health*, 45 (January, 1955), p. 8.

The Setting and the Problem

Thus layer upon layer of government exists in many sections of metropolitan areas.[13]

The numerous and overlapping units present a local governmental pattern that is inadequate for metropolitan needs. Public activities are splintered among many governmental units, and each of them is legally free to act independently on certain matters that may have substantial effects beyond its borders in other parts of the metropolitan area. The various types of local governments were mostly conceived in a pre-metropolitan period for non-metropolitan conditions. Their use in metropolitan areas largely represents improvisation rather than a carefully formulated system fitted to particular metropolitan situations.

The Metropolitan Problem: A Series of Problems

The metropolitan problem has become more acute in a setting of continuing growth of metropolitan areas in number, population, territorial size and governmental complexity. Although its magnitude and aggravation are generally greatest in the most populous or the medium-sized areas, the problem exists in virtually all metropolitan situations. The persistence of the metropolitan trend indicates that the less populous metropolitan areas, and even embryonic ones, may need to make changes soon to avoid comparable conditions.

The basis of the problem is the absence of general local governmental organizations broad enough to cope with metropolitan matters. There is a lack of area-wide governmental jurisdictions that can effectively provide and finance services, that can plan and regulate and that are constructed to facilitate adequate accountability to the metropolitan public for their actions. The metropolitan problem thus is in fact a series of major problems.

Inadequate Governmental Structure

Prominent in the series of problems is the inadequacy of governmental organization. Current metropolitan needs have outmoded substantial parts of the local governmental system, which was largely conceived

---

[13] For specific examples *see* U.S. Bureau of the Census, Governments Division, *Local Government in Metropolitan Areas*, State and Local Government Special Studies No. 36 (Washington: 1954), pp. 15–24. A more detailed, earlier listing is contained in U.S. Bureau of the Census, Governments Division, *Governmental Units Overlying City Areas*, Governmental Organization Series No. 3 (Washington: 1947).

in the eighteenth century. "The basic structure of local government, by and large," notes a recent commentator, "fails miserably to reflect the best that is known concerning governmental structure. . . . We cannot overlook the fact that our failure to devise improved local and metropolitan structures of government results in the less efficient use of the supply [of public money]."[14] Adjustments have taken place in some types of local governments, such as certain cities and counties, but the alterations have not been sufficient to handle the mounting difficulties. The rapid rise of large and small special district governments in metropolitan areas is indicative of the insufficiency of the general, traditional local units.

An overwhelming proportion of local governments functioning in metropolitan areas have decidedly limited jurisdictions. In the relatively few instances where a local government does embrace most or all of the metropolitan area, it usually is still inadequate. Although its jurisdiction is large enough, its powers are not. This is particularly noticeable of many counties and some special districts, which are legally restricted in their activities. Almost always the metropolitan area lacks a general metropolitan government. The need is not necessarily for each such area to have a single local government, but one or more governmental jurisdictions of sufficient territory and authority are required.

Interest in metropolitan area reform is considerable today. Satisfactory legal means of implementing the interest, however, have lagged. Ordinarily, the state constitutional provisions and state laws that can be utilized in metropolitan reorganization are difficult to employ. They are in a number of instances deterrents or insurmountable obstacles to such activity. Many of them were formulated for use in more limited areas, in a period before extensive metropolitan expansion occurred. In some states, moreover, the range of optional legal possibilities is very narrow.

Service and Regulatory Defects

Service and control deficiencies are another part of the series of problems. These deficiencies are numerous because the many governments involved operate in only limited portions of the metropolitan areas and provide varying levels of services and regulation. Although some of

[14] Lennox L. Moak, "Financial Problems of the Metropolitan Areas," in Tax Institute, *Financing Metropolitan Government* (Princeton: 1955), p. 6. Mr. Moak's article contains an excellent, brief discussion of several problems considered in this section.

The Setting and the Problem

their policies affect metropolitan developments, they often are made on the basis of what is advantageous for the restricted segment of the area each government occupies. As a result, services and regulation are uneven, and area-wide approaches in attacking common difficulties are lacking or slow in materializing.

The relative seriousness of specific service and regulatory deficiencies varies in individual areas.[15] Generally, however, since easy movement of people and goods is basic to the well-being of metropolitan areas, defects in transportation are the most acute. Included may be inferior conditions of a few or many related components: mass transit service, airport and port facilities, traffic regulation and accident prevention, street, highway, and freeway systems, railway and trucking terminals, and private car parking accommodations. Shortcomings in sanitation often are critical. Haphazard, uncoordinated methods of disposing of sewage and garbage bring water pollution and affect public health and recreation. In recent years air pollution has become more serious.

Public health activities to prevent spread of disease are scattered chaotically among many governments in metropolitan areas. Individually their staffs and equipment range greatly in quality. Planning and zoning controls, enacted independently in localities without regard for over-all metropolitan development, may result in many ill effects, including substandard housing and blighted, undeveloped land. Numerous other deficiencies often exist. They occur in civil defense, education, libraries and law enforcement. Still others appear in fire prevention and protection, water supply and distribution, drainage, and park and recreation facilities. *Project East River*, a recent study of civil defense prepared for the national government, commented upon the fragmentary rendering of functions in metropolitan areas. It concluded:

> The use of traditional [local governmental boundary] lines creates extraordinary complications where normal governmental functions are involved. The observance of the same boundaries creates even greater difficulties when an effort is made to develop an integrated operational plan for civil defense of a metropolitan area.[16]

There is much service and much regulation in metropolitan areas, but frequently they are uneconomic and ill-fitted to the tasks at hand.

---

[15] Additional details on particular weaknesses are presented in Paul Studenski, *The Government of Metropolitan Areas in the United States* (New York: National Municipal League, 1930), pp. 30–37, and Victor Jones, *Metropolitan Government* (Chicago: University of Chicago Press, 1942), pp. 52–72. The shortcomings discussed in these early general works usually have increased in intensity in more recent years.

[16] Associated Universities, Inc., *Project East River*, General Report, Part I (New York: 1952), p. 32.

Financial Inequalities and Weaknesses

Financial inequalities and shortcomings are also part of the series of problems. There are wide variances in different sections of metropolitan areas between service needs and financial resources. The policy of providing city-wide services on the basis of need rather than the fiscal resources of each block, precinct or ward is not extended in the great majority of instances to metropolitan areas.[17] Instead, the individual governmental unit relies upon a small amount of territory for its local financial resources. Thus some units are wealthy but have relatively few needs; others are extremely poor and have extensive needs. Such disparity between needs and resources is particularly apparent in the central cities, which must furnish services to many non-residents but cannot tap the financial resources of the localities in which these people reside. The broad variations between needs and resources make for gross inequalities in financial burdens.

The financial situation is further complicated by existing tax and revenue systems and debt limitations. Taxes and revenue sources of various kinds of local governments often are severely restricted. This results from long-standing state laws and constitutional provisions whose reasons for establishment may have been forgotten for many years. Debt limitations imposed by state laws and constitutions also are common. Often they are unrealistic because they are based on assessed valuations of real property which have not been adjusted sufficiently and because the relative importance of the property tax has declined. These limitations apply to governmental areas that, as a rule, are highly restricted territorially. Consequently, "large areas have been immobilized because of the unavailability of borrowing power in one or two relatively minor, but key, political subdivisions. Conversely, in some areas, improvident use of borrowing powers has caused the more conservative neighbors to recoil from intimate association with the prodigals."[18]

The problem of a sufficient financial base was emphasized in 1955 by the *Economic Report of the President* in its statement that "many communities are prevented from utilizing their financing capacities by outmoded tax-rate or debt limits."[19] An adequate tax and revenue system

---

[17] Jones, *Metropolitan Government*, p. 73.

[18] Moak, "Financial Problems of the Metropolitan Areas," p. 8.

[19] *Economic Report of the President* (Washington: Government Printing Office, 1955), p. 63.

The Setting and the Problem

and debt limitation arrangement are especially important to the conversion of an existing unit to metropolitan status or to the creation of a new metropolitan government. They are also basic to the adequate performance by local units of strictly local functions.

Not least important in the financial situation of metropolitan areas is the matter of grants-in-aid from the state and national governments. In some instances such grants have fostered improved governmental organization in metropolitan areas. In others they have had the effect of bolstering uneconomic and inefficient governmental units. Grants-in-aid are a powerful implement that can have substantial impact in supporting or hindering metropolitan reorganization.

Deficiencies in Citizen Control

Finally, popular control of government is a crucial part of "the metropolitan problem." Citizen control over metropolitan areas is inadequate and ineffective. People living within many sections of a metropolitan area reside in numerous governmental jurisdictions and are confronted with an extremely large number of issues and personalities on which they are to form judgments. Conscientious citizens probably are able to stay sufficiently well informed about the activities of the national government, the state government, and one or two local governments, but the proliferation of local units has made the total task impossible. The scattering of public authority and responsibility and the resulting complexity overburden local residents. The existing demands in many segments of metropolitan areas greatly exceed the span of attention that citizens can be expected to maintain.

The pattern of many governments functioning in portions of metropolitan areas resembles a circus containing far more than the usual three rings. Public confusion, disinterest and cynicism mount because the time needed to watch over and control so many independent governmental operations is so large.

Citizen control in metropolitan areas is inadequate and ineffective in another important way. Even if residents were able to fulfill the herculean role of observing and controlling the numerous governments in whose jurisdictions they live, this would be insufficient. Residents can make a decision at elections about such functions as transportation or sewage disposal, for example—but it is usually binding on only a limited amount of the metropolitan territory. Generally there is no method of metropolitan-wide electoral participation in matters of metropolitan scope. Without it, no adequate citizen control of metropolitan areas can exist.

Moreover, the inadequacy and ineffectiveness of popular control breed political irresponsibility. The absence of formal, direct channels of action that are usable throughout a metropolitan area does not preclude the establishment of more indirect ones. Many people in a metropolitan area have no official voice in the governmental affairs of the city where they work because they live elsewhere; some of them, nevertheless, exert significant influence on its government through participation in civic, business and labor organizations that concern themselves with the city's policies and deal with its officials. This is especially evident among numerous suburban dwellers who work in the central city, but the reverse situation is not unknown. In either circumstance the degree of political irresponsibility can be high because the activities, whether friendly or antagonistic to the city government, are not conditioned by local residence and the power and accountability of direct action.

The complex of difficulties that make up the metropolitan problem can be substantially overcome. But to do so requires establishment of general governmental jurisdictions of metropolitan scope—jurisdictions that are representative of the people directly affected and are accountable and responsive to them.

Part Two

THE METROPOLITAN RECORD:
APPROACHES TO SOLVING THE PROBLEM

1. *Annexation*
2. *City-County Consolidation*
3. *City-County Separation*
4. *Federation*
5. *Functional Transfers and Joint Efforts*
6. *Metropolitan Special Districts*

PART TWO

The Metropolitan Record: Approaches to Solving the Problem

SIX methods of attacking the metropolitan problem have received the most frequent use or advocacy. They are annexation, city-county consolidation, city-county separation, federation, transfer and joint handling of functions, and metropolitan special districts. In this second part of the study, each of these six methods is analyzed and appraised, and important local illustrations are considered. Particular attention is given to ways in which actions of the states have affected actual or attempted use of these approaches.

1. ANNEXATION

Annexation, the absorption of territory by a city, always has been the most common method for adjusting local governmental boundaries in urban and metropolitan areas.[1] The nature of its earlier use, however, has largely changed in the present century, and consequently in recent decades annexation has not had large-scale, general significance in solving the metropolitan problem. Until the late years of the nineteenth century, its importance was far greater. Up to that time many of what are now the central cities of metropolitan areas gained large numbers of square miles through annexation. The process was principally responsible for transforming most of these cities from small-sized incorporations into major urban centers. It enabled them to become the focal points of metropolitan areas and prevented the subsequent rise of numerous additional small cities.

The Nature of Early Annexation

The growth in area of many cities was spectacular until about the beginning of the twentieth century. A few illustrations of the increase

[1] The word "city" rather than "municipality" is generally used in this study to designate incorporated places variously known as cities, towns in other than New England states, villages and boroughs. "Municipality" is reserved principally for instances in which "city" might be interpreted too narrowly.

from the date of incorporation to 1900 will indicate the extensiveness of expansion by means of annexation. Chicago grew from 10½ to 190 square miles, Boston from 4½ to 38½, and Pittsburgh from half a square mile to 28. Minneapolis increased from 8 to 53 square miles and St. Louis from ½ mile to 61 square miles.[2]

Large Annexations

Annexation before 1900 had several conspicuous characteristics. The most prominent was that numerous cities absorbed much area, frequently through relatively few actions. Predominantly, the annexed areas were unincorporated, but annexation of incorporated communities, generally small in population and land, was not extraordinary. Territory annexed was usually not intensively urbanized, at least not nearly to the degree typical in more recent years in settlements adjacent to central cities.

Liberal Laws

Many annexations were completed without a separate popular vote in the annexed areas. They were accomplished through special acts of the legislature, through general legislative acts that were in reality special laws because of the detailed classification of cities, and through legislation stipulating a combined vote in the city and in the area to be annexed. Even when annexation acts called for individual consent of the localities involved, they were replaced at times by new laws ordering annexation because local approval had not been forthcoming under the previous legislation. Moreover, the areas of some cities grew through use of annexation and another method of area reorganization at different times, or by annexation as part of another method. The experience of St. Louis is a good example of a city that employed both procedures. The city annexed unincorporated territory in 1822, 1841 and 1851, and the City of Carondolet in 1870, all by means of special legislative acts. Then, in 1876, a county-wide vote favored separation of the City of St. Louis from St. Louis County; the city at this time annexed forty-three square miles to its corporate limits, more than tripling its size.[3]

[2] R. D. McKenzie, *The Metropolitan Community* (New York: McGraw-Hill, 1933), pp. 336–337. The figures have been rounded and include both land and water areas for comparative purposes because many of the earlier records did not separate them.

[3] City-county separation and city-county consolidation, which are distinct area reorganization approaches, are considered in detail in subsequent sections.

The Decline of Annexation

The complexion of annexation began to change drastically around the turn of the twentieth century, at the very time when metropolitan areas were becoming numerous. Once metropolitan areas arose, and as they came to contain more and more people, land and incorporated communities, use of the device fell increasingly behind the need for expansion of municipal boundaries. Subsequently, annexation has never regained the pre-eminent position it had held among area reorganization methods.

Smaller in Number and in Area

In general, from about 1900 to the end of World War II annexations dwindled in number, in total area absorbed, and in the average size of annexed areas. For example, in the decade 1920–1930 substantially less total territory was annexed than in 1890–1900, and a group of representative cities annexed only one-fifteenth as much area as thirty years before.

In the 1920's, for numerous central cities, especially in the more populous metropolitan areas, use of annexation became completely dormant or small scale, and when it occurred almost always involved unincorporated territory. At the same time, new incorporations of suburbs in metropolitan areas became very widespread. Central city annexations were even fewer in the following decade. By the time of World War II, annexation as a device to integrate the governmental organization of metropolitan areas seemed of little current significance.

Increased Suburbanization

The simultaneous decline of annexation and the rise and growth of metropolitan areas were not simply coincidental. People increasingly settled beyond the limits of central cities. Outlying sectors grew in territorial size and in distance from the central cities because individuals were able to make intensive use of technological improvements, such as private automobiles. As more people came to locate in them, the feeling of community spirit or local home rule grew. Many areas incorporated and others became populous, unincorporated communities.

More Restrictive Legal Provisions

Changes in many state laws and constitutional provisions were a major element in decreasing annexations. As extensive urbanization of territory beyond central cities continued, residents of incorporated suburbs and unincorporated communities successfully demanded legal alterations to make annexation (or consolidation, as the process is termed in some states) more difficult.

Many of the legal bases concerned with annexation were revised in one, two or three ways. The procedure became highly complicated. The people in outlying areas were granted the exclusive authority to initiate annexation. They were endowed with a conclusive veto over annexation proposals by receiving the power to vote on the matter separately from central city residents. The requirement of a separate vote became especially prevalent in procedures relating to annexation or consolidation of one city to another. In some instances, where legal bases were not revised, the suburban representation in the state legislatures became sufficiently strong to block attempts to pass special acts calling for annexation of a city or a populous unincorporated community.

Changing Conditions and Shifting Interests

Other important causes contributed to the decline of annexation. As metropolitan areas grew in territory, some of them crossed county boundaries and state lines. Many state laws did not provide for cross-county annexations, and consequently very few of these occurred. There were no interstate annexations because such actions would have necessitated one state giving up territory to another. Another important contributor to the decline of annexation was the growing resentment of suburban residents to the complete obliteration of all autonomy of their localities. Because of all these legal obstacles and because of the mounting opposition to annexation, the people of a number of metropolitan areas turned their attention to other means of area reorganization.

The Post World War II Revival

The final year of World War II witnessed a resurgence in the use of annexation. One hundred and fifty-two cities of at least 5,000 population annexed territory in 1945. Eighty-nine of them contained more

The Metropolitan Record: Annexation

than 10,000 people each; they represented a virtual doubling of the average number of comparable cities that annexed annually from 1935 through 1939. Annexation continued at an increased rate in 1946, when there were 259 annexing cities. In this year the number with more than 10,000 population exceeded the five-year average of the late 1930's by more than three times.

Some observers regarded the revival of annexation as a temporary trend, resulting from a backlog of deferred action. The annexations now taking place, they held, would have been spread out over earlier years of the decade if the war had not deflected public attention to larger issues. But that judgment soon had to be withdrawn. The number of cities of 5,000 or more people completing annexations continued to spiral in the following year, approaching the 300 mark. After a slight decrease in 1948, the total crossed 300 in 1949 and moved near to 400 in 1950. Following a recession in 1951 to about the level of two years before, the total of annexing cities exceeded 400 in each of the three years from 1952 through 1954. Approximately one of every six cities of 5,000 or more population in the United States annexed some territory in each of these three years. In 1954 six times as many cities of more than 10,000 people annexed than in the 1935–1939 period.

Much of the revitalized annexation activity that has spanned the decade since 1945 has occurred in metropolitan areas. Approximately one-half of all central cities of metropolitan areas have annexed territory during these years. Many cities in such areas other than the central cities also have completed annexations. The annexation movement, however, has not resulted in the transformation of central cities into governmental jurisdictions of metropolitan scope.

Differences from Earlier Development

The postwar annexation trend resembles that of the nineteenth century in terms of the large number of participating cities. It differs, however, in other significant respects. Many cities have completed annexations in recent years, but generally they have annexed territory of small size. In metropolitan areas where central cities completed annexations in the seven years from 1948 through 1954, most of them annexed territory ranging in total from a fraction of a square mile to a few square miles each.[4] In many instances numerous successful actions were neces-

[4] Data on the size of individual annexations are not available for 1945 through 1947.

sary under difficult state laws to annex a very small total amount of territory. In addition, practically all areas were unincorporated when they were annexed. The annexation or consolidation of one city to another has been virtually unknown in metropolitan areas in this recent period. At the same time there have been many new small incorporations. As a consequence, some central cities, such as Minneapolis, are completely hemmed in by other incorporated communities that are protected from merger attempts by state legal provisions requiring their separate approval.

TABLE 5

A DECADE OF ANNEXATION ACTIVITY, 1945–1954

YEAR	ALL CITIES OVER 5,000		CITIES OVER 10,000		CITIES OF 5,000 TO 10,000	
	Total no. of annexing cities	Total no. of square miles annexed	Total no. of annexing cities	Total no. of square miles annexed	Total no. of annexing cities	Total no. of square miles annexed
1954	410	325	289	288	121	37
1953	434	282	266	228	168	54
1952	402	277	247	244	155	33
1951	309	230	211	213	98	17
1950	382	200	223	173	159	27
1949	301	272	188	243	113	29
1948	288	146	193	129	95	17
1947	298	....	170	....	128	....
1946	259	....	154	....	105	....
1945	152	....	89	....	63	....

Source: John C. Bollens, "Metropolitan and Fringe Area Developments in 1954," *Municipal Year Book: 1955* (Chicago: International City Managers' Association, 1955), p. 42, and previous articles by the same author in the editions of the *Year Book* published from 1949 through 1954. The totals for square miles annexed have been rounded. As of 1950, there were 1,233 cities of more than 10,000 population and 1,093 cities of 5,000 to 10,000 population.

There have been some major exceptions to the general pattern of small annexations by central cities of metropolitan areas. These exceptions are important both because of their territorial extent and because certain of their features explain why such accomplishments are not more customary. Since 1948, Atlanta, Dallas, Houston, and San Antonio have annexed approximately eighty square miles each. An addition twenty-one central cities have each annexed from ten to sixty-seven square miles. In all, about one of every eight central cities has annexed such sizable territory.

The Features of Large Annexations

Two features have characterized these large annexations in a period dominated by small annexations. First, most of them materialized under one of five types of legal provisions, none of which gave the residents or property owners of the territory under consideration for annexation a separate, controlling vote. (1) The city council of the annexing city passed an annexation ordinance. (2) The people of the city undertaking the annexation effort voted in favor of the proposal. (3) The election results in the city and in the area to be annexed were counted together. (4) The state legislature passed a special act. (5) A court rendered a decision favorable to annexation. Because of the more liberal nature of these legal processes, central cities were able to accomplish large-scale

TABLE 6

CENTRAL CITIES ANNEXING THE LARGEST AREAS, 1948–1954

1950 population class of central city	Total square miles annexed	1950 population class of central city	Total square miles annexed
500,000–1,000,000		*100,000–250,000*	
Houston	83.27	Austin	13.78
Milwaukee	19.88	Corpus Christi	15.04
		El Paso	51.77
250,000–500,000		Norfolk	11.16
Atlanta	82.00	Oklahoma City	22.15
Birmingham	16.08	Tampa	46.25
Dallas	79.80	Wichita	11.24
Fort Worth	13.43		
Kansas City, Mo.	67.31	*50,000–100,000*	
Louisville	11.04	Albuquerque	35.57
Memphis	23.62	Amarillo	10.52
San Antonio	80.90	Madison	10.56
San Diego	21.97	Roanoke	11.83
Seattle	16.47	San Angelo	21.70
		Waterloo	12.99

annexations through comparatively few annexation actions. Houston for example, gained seventy-nine square miles through a single annexation.

Second, the central cities that annexed large amounts of area usually have not been located near large numbers of incorporated suburbs. Most of them were in small, medium-sized, or fast growing metropolitan areas that at the time of annexation possessed much more unincorporated territory and far fewer cities than the most populous metroplitan areas. For example, the Dallas metropolitan area in 1952 had nineteen cities, Houston had sixteen and San Antonio eight. In contrast, the Pittsburgh metropolitan area had 181 and the Chicago area 192.

The more liberal annexation laws utilized in completing annexations of large unincorporated areas could not have been used by most of these central cities in annexation efforts concerning another city. A separate vote would have been required. Thus the large annexations by central cities have generally been completed under legal procedures not requiring a separate vote in the area to be annexed and have occurred in metropolitan areas in which considerable unincorporated territory still existed adjacent to the central cities. One or both of these favorable conditions were unavailable to many central cities making small annexations or none at all.

Although these large annexations have been important, their value as approaches to establishing an adequate metropolitan governmental organization is limited. Every one of the central cities that annexed a large amount of territory in recent years still encompasses only a relatively small part of the metropolitan area. For example, the four annexation leaders—Atlanta, Dallas, Houston and San Antonio, each of which annexed about eighty square miles—currently include within their boundaries less than one-fourth of the metropolitan area as determined by the Census Bureau. Moreover, subsequent to the completion of large annexations, some central cities, including Albuquerque and Houston, have undertaken investigations of other methods of area reorganization. Their more recent actions recognize that annexation alone is not ordinarily a sufficient answer to the metropolitan problem.

Greatest Usefulness in Fringe Areas

In recent years the annexation trend has had its greatest general significance as a means of resolving problems involving a city and its adjacent unincorporated urban fringe rather than as a method of attaining a metropolitan government. Annexation has been unable to keep pace with the territorial expansion of metropolitan areas. Its applicability has become largely restricted to unincorporated territory under even the most favorable legal provisions. Interest has increased in other area reorganization approaches that preserve a degree of autonomy in established localities which become parts of a metropolitan government.

The decline in general importance of annexation as a metropolitan device does not mean that it has become inconsequential in all metropolitan situations. In certain circumstances it may be the preferred approach, or it may be a desirable supplement to other approaches, or it may be the only method used or available.

The Metropolitan Record: Annexation

Annexation has been having considerable effect in parts of metropolitan areas in solving difficulties that cannot be ignored pending more comprehensive solutions. Most basically, it has provided a method for central and other cities in metropolitan areas individually to assume jurisdiction over neighboring areas that usually have many deficiencies in services and controls. Such defects are harmful to both the fringe dwellers and the city inhabitants.

Through annexing fringe areas, cities have been able to correct many of these unsatisfactory conditions. They have brought improvements in jerry-built developments that had inadequate sanitation, mud-rut streets in incompleted subdivisions, and intermixtures of industrial, commercial and residential uses. They have eliminated havens for vice and gambling and wiped out fire hazards that had existed at the pre-annexation borders. Thus they have eradicated many shortcomings of the fringe that previously spilled over the official city limits and harassed city residents.[5] Moreover, annexation of fringe areas stops controversy over whether it is equitable for counties to provide municipal-type functions to fringes without making added charges. Various cities have argued that, as heavy contributors to the county treasury, they subsidize the performance of such functions by counties in urban fringes.[6]

Annexation also has been important because it has contributed to preventing further increase in governmental complexity and to reducing existing complexities in particular sections of metropolitan areas. By bringing unincorporated territory within the boundaries of a city, it has removed the opportunity for small cities and small single purpose special districts to be established. In addition, annexation has eliminated many small and costly special districts, each of which supplied functions subsequently performed by the city. Moreover, when accomplished before an area is heavily urbanized, it has provided the means for a city, through land-use control, to effect orderly development in harmony with the city's older sections.

Need for Changes in Annexation Laws

Annexation, however, has fallen far behind the expansion of metropolitan areas, and it has not even been keeping up with fringe area

[5] John C. Bollens, "Fringe Area Conditions and Relations," *Public Management*, 32 (March, 1950), p. 51.

[6] Richard Graves, "Fringe Areas Should Pay Their Own Way," *Public Management*, 34 (February, 1952), pp. 30–33.

growth. Difficult and cumbersome annexation legal provisions frequently have made the attempts of cities to absorb annoying urban fringes hard or impossible. Fresno, California, for example, had to complete 150 annexation actions successfully during seven recent years in order to obtain slightly more than five square miles of fringe area. If annexation is to be a truly effective device in dealing with urban fringe difficulties, major changes will be required in the annexation laws of many states.

Numerous annexation laws are unworkable or burdensome to use in fringe area situations because the fringe residents have the sole right to initiate the proceedings or the power to vote separately on the question, or both these authorizations. The proposition is not decided on the basis of the needs of the entire urban area, of which the city and the fringe are parts. The city thus is in an impossible position if it cannot persuade the fringe of the advantages it will obtain from annexation. Such efforts at persuasion often consume many years; meanwhile conditions in the fringe area grow worse and detrimentally affect the entire area occupied by the city and the fringe. Many times the efforts are unsuccessful. Under these circumstances the city is powerless.

Many annexation laws should be made less stringent. They should be altered so that fringe residents and fringe property owners do not control the usability of this method of area change. Such renovations will abolish the dominant position of the relatively few in the fringe regardless of the effect the fringe is having on the very many in the city. They will furnish the means for the paramount public interest to prevail over the lesser interest in matters affecting both the city and the fringe.

The procedural steps involved in a number of annexation laws also should be simplified. Too often they contain tortuous, easily misunderstood or obscure provisions. Eliminating these procedural defects will permit quicker and more certain use of the process.

The Alternatives

No single best method of annexation is uniformly applicable to all states. States differ too widely in economic, social, and political characteristics to make this possible. However, various existing and proposed methods may usefully be presented, and certain questions, guidelines and facts can be offered for consideration and analysis in individual states.

One procedure used in some states is for the state legislature to pass acts that enlarge the boundaries of a city so that they encompass the fringe. This method produces results, but several questions suggest themselves. Should the legislature make the decisions on such matters? Do many states have numerous constitutional obstacles to this kind of action? Do other state legislatures feel that annexations can be handled better in another way?

A second possibility is to require a vote of the city residents only—as in Missouri home rule cities and some Texas home rule cities—or an over-all, combined popular vote of the city and the fringe. Again, the system produces results, but its advocates may confront these questions. Is it equitable? Does it permit the city to override the fringe in instances where the facts do not warrant annexation?

Another series of approaches is based on the conviction that the merits of annexation cannot be decided in an election. One such approach, used in Ohio, calls for annexation proposals to be considered by the county governing body. Another, available in New Mexico, provides for a seven-member board of arbitration, composed of city and fringe residents. A third, operative in the Canadian Province of Ontario and frequently advocated for adoption in various states, consists of referral of the question to a state administrative agency possessing quasi-judicial powers. A fourth, identified with Virginia, involves a special annexation court of three circuit judges. Is determination by such groups preferable to decisions through combined city-fringe or city elections or by the state legislatures? Is one of these four methods more desirable than the others?

An entirely different method, followed by many home rule cities in Texas, is to allow annexation through ordinance action of the city council. Is this approach justifiable, some observers ask, or too advantageous to cities?

Annexation in Texas

It is appropriate to analyze in detail the annexation development in Texas, where municipalities have annexed the largest amount of territory in the period since World War II, and in Virginia, where the most sustained use of annexation in the present century has occurred.

The key factor in the extensiveness of the Texas movement is the authority conferred on home rule cities. The state constitution was amended in 1912 to authorize voters in cities of more than 5,000 population to amend or adopt local charters and become home rule cities. In the following year a general state enabling act was passed, enumerating a number of home rule powers. One of its sections provided that a home rule city could annex adjacent territory according to rules written into its local charter.

Broad Grant to Home Rule Cities

Through these constitutional and statutory provisions and through later judicial decisions, home rule cities have obtained broad discretion to specify in their charters the annexation procedure they will follow. For example, the Texas Supreme Court in 1938 stressed that "The Home Rule Amendment and the Enabling Act transferred to the specified cities through the agency of their qualified voters the same power which the Legislature had heretofore possessed to change territorial boundaries."[7] The major restriction upon the locally determined process is that a home rule city cannot by its action alone annex another home rule city or a general law municipality eligible to adopt a charter because it has more than 5,000 population. Although the State Supreme Court has never decided the point, the lower courts have judged that, similarly, a home rule city cannot unilaterally annex a general law municipality containing less than 5,000 inhabitants.[8]

Within the framework restricting the annexation right of home rule cities to unincorporated territory, they have much freedom if they decide to exercise it. Annexations may be of any size or shape so long as part of the territory is contiguous. They may not be challenged in the courts on the basis of the wisdom or purpose of the action. Since the power of home rule cities to annex is legislative in nature, completed annexations may in general be attacked in the courts only by the state, on the ground that the broad statutory authority has been exceeded.

Primarily Used in Fringe Areas

Although home rule cities have much latitude in annexation, it is a device largely utilized in urban fringe area situations. In view of the

[7] 116 S.W. (2) 469 (1938).

[8] Incorporated places in Texas can consolidate, but the actions must be taken under general state laws requiring mutual consent and not under local provisions established in the charter of simply one of them. There have been very few consolidations in recent years. Several have formally involved the dissolution of one city on the decision of its voters, followed by annexation of the reconverted, unincorporated territory by another city.

stipulations that the territory annexed must be adjacent and must not include incorporated communities, it has not been a widely applicable method of solving the metropolitan problem. As the research staff of the Texas Legislative Council has stated: "Texas annexation laws [in operation in both home rule and general law cities] were designed principally to enable cities to deal with developing fringe in areas contiguous to their boundaries. Development in standard metropolitan areas does not usually follow this simple pattern. New growth, including population concentrations and industry, may be in communities [some of which incorporate and thus have the power to withstand absorption] . . . miles from the city's corporate limits and not contiguous to them."[9]

Two Procedures

In writing annexation provisions into local charters, Texas home rule cities have adopted one of two procedures. Sixty-five of the 120 home rule cities, including most of the more populous urban centers, permit annexation of unincorporated territory without the consent of the voters or property owners of the land involved. Most of them, including Austin, Dallas, Houston and San Antonio, can annex by council ordinance. Some, such as Corpus Christi and Fort Worth, require majority approval of the city's voters.[10] In neither case does the area to be annexed have a formal part in the proceedings. The charters of the remaining fifty-five home rule cities, including Amarillo, Galveston and Wichita Falls, call for consent of the voters of the areas under consideration for annexation. Action usually is completed by council ordinance of the annexing city. The annexation procedure operating in this group of home rule cities is quite similar to that present in Texas general law cities, towns and villages. The latter, also, must obtain majority consent of the voters of the territory considered. The major difference is that ordinarily home rule cities do not legally limit themselves to annexations of not more than one-half mile in width— a restriction imposed on general law cities by the state legislature.

Most of the total area annexed in Texas since 1945 has been obtained by home rule cities whose charters permit unilateral annexation action

[9] Texas Legislative Council, *Municipal Annexation*, Staff Report (Austin: 1954), p. 53.

[10] The latter procedure is in effect similar to the one operating in home rule cities of Missouri, where the State Supreme Court held in 1950 that such cities can annex unincorporated, adjoining territory through a favorable popular vote in the city on a proposed charter amendment.

either by council ordinance or by approval of the city voters. Their need to use annexation has been great because they are generally the most populous cities in the state and have been confronted with very pressing problems in the adjoining fringes. But many other municipalities have similar difficulties, different mainly in degree of intensity. The wide disparity between the annexation records of these home rule cities and those of other home rule and general law cities can be attributed largely to the roles assigned under the respective legal procedures to people in the outlying territory. In many instances the decisive factor is whether separate approval must be obtained in the area to be annexed.

Absorption of Many Fringe Areas

Use by home rule cities of the authority to annex through council ordinance or through approval by the city voters has brought both helpful and disadvantageous results. Without question, a very important consequence has been that many fringe areas containing service and regulatory deficiencies have been brought under the full and permanent jurisdiction of a general urban local government. This is a very large accomplishment and one that is substantially lacking in numerous other states.

Defensive and Competitive Actions

Other effects—some general and others less frequent—have raised problems. One is the development of defensive and competitive races to annex or incorporate. These races are the product of three factors: the annexation process available to home rule cities, the judicially imposed limitation of such power, and the nature of the incorporation law. Any city of more than 5,000 people may place in its locally adopted charter a procedure that annexations can be undertaken by its exclusive action. The courts have held that incorporated places cannot be annexed without their consent. Any area containing 200 qualified voters can incorporate.

By passing an annexation ordinance on first reading, many home rule cities are able to lay claim to unincorporated territory until they are ready to finish the annexation. This prevents the area from either incorporating or being annexed by another municipality. However, if an area containing a relatively few residents starts an incorporation proceeding in advance of the beginning of an annexation by a city, and subsequently completes the process, it is immune from annexation. Such

The Metropolitan Record: Annexation

incorporation may mean the conversion of an unincorporated area with few services into an incorporated place still lacking adequate services but legally protected from annexation. At times two cities and an unincorporated area may act with as much secrecy and speed as possible to gain the advantage. Within a comparatively short period a long series of annexations and incorporations may be set into motion.

This "chain reaction" pattern occurred in the Dallas-Fort Worth area in recent years and was later partially repeated in the Houston and San Antonio areas. Dallas and Fort Worth became very active in annexing during the 1940's. In 1948 Dallas extended its limits down a narrow strip of land to absorb certain industrial developments situated adjacent to Grand Prairie, then a city of less than five square miles and of approximately 15,000 people. This action prompted Grand Prairie to adopt a home rule charter that allowed the city council to annex. By 1953 it had laid claim, through first reading ordinances, to more than 100 square miles in two counties. Its proposed boundaries touched those of four cities, including Dallas, whose westward growth was blocked. They passed around two sides of the new multi-million dollar international airport between Dallas and Fort Worth, and encompassed an unincorporated community of 3,000 population that had rejected incorporation a few months before.[11] Concurrently, numerous other incorporated places in Dallas County also expanded by means of annexation. One of them, with about 2,600 people and bordered by Grand Prairie after the latter's annexation activity, added twenty-seven square miles. New incorporations likewise materialized. In 1953 alone four new towns in the county incorporated.

Annexations and incorporations may proceed in cyclical fashion under the broadly discretionary rules that are available. Suburban communities incorporate to avoid annexation. Cities annex in order to prevent incorporations and to preclude other incorporated areas from annexing particular territories. The cycle begins with either incorporation or annexation, and the first one used may lead to use of the second and further employment of the first.

Other Results

Another outcome of permitting home rule cities to make an exclusive judgment about annexing is that some of them have avoided the absorp-

[11] J. M. Claunch, "Land Grabbing—Texas Style," *National Municipal Review*, 42 (November, 1953), p. 495.

tion of certain fringe areas, even when requested to do so by the fringe residents. Such sectors may lack adequate taxpaying ability to finance a reasonable share of the cost of municipal services but nevertheless constitute problem areas to the adjacent cities. Selective annexation has brought forth the critical comment that cities practicing it want to annex well-to-do developments but by-pass poorer neighboring fringes. Also contributing to selective annexation have been widespread and often successful attempts by business organizations to obtain a guarantee from a city, before locating in its vicinity, of immunity from annexation for from one to thirty-five years.

An additional result of unilateral city action is that annexations sometimes have been undertaken without adequate prior consideration. For example, a minority of Texas home rule cities that annexed in recent years utilized planning services in studying proposed annexations, and only a few conducted careful investigations of the areas. Moreover, city officials themselves agree that a common abuse of the annexation procedure is the inability of numerous cities to provide satisfactory services to large amounts of territory that have been absorbed.[12]

The home rule annexation power in Texas thus is a potent instrument that has done much to lessen the fringe area difficulty, but not all of its effects have been beneficial. In the words of one analyst in the state:

> ... a close examination of the facts of specific [annexation] projects will sometimes reveal, however [fitting] such development generally may be, that home-rule power to annex can be used abusively, harshly, as a cloak for personal ambition, and even, it has been insinuated, as a pawn in industrial rivalry. On the other hand, that much of the opposition is moved by particularist selfish motivation cannot be denied ... municipal growth calls for the exercise of wise statesmanship that understands and respects legitimate diversity and even conflict of interest and that ... undertakes as its highest task the reconciliation of these varying interests for the common good.[13]

Annexation in Virginia

The most consistent use of annexation in this century has been in Virginia. It has resulted directly from assigning such determinations to a specially constituted court. The state constitution of 1902 prohibited the previous practice of annexation by special legislation and directed the legislature to enact general laws on the matter. A deadlock soon

---

[12] These points are discussed in Texas Legislative Council, *Municipal Annexation*, pp. 28, 31, 38.

[13] August O. Spain, "Politics of Recent Municipal Annexation in Texas," *Southwestern Social Science Quarterly*, 30 (June, 1949), p. 28.

developed in the legislature as to whether the extension of municipal boundaries should be decided by judicial process or by popular vote, but in 1904 the legislature adopted an annexation law providing for judicial determination of annexation proposals. Its constitutionality was upheld in 1906 by the State Supreme Court of Appeals, which rejected a contention that the statute illegally delegated legislative powers to the judiciary.

Decisions by the Judiciary

The basic features of the law call for selection of circuit court judges who determine under legislatively prescribed terms when the boundaries of cities and towns should be readjusted. These features have remained the same since their original enactment. Most of the amendments adopted have related either to developments that were not initially anticipated or to alterations in standards to be utilized by the courts. Other amendments have increased the number of judges deciding an annexation proceeding, changed the circuits from which judges are chosen, and substituted the chief justice of the State Supreme Court of Appeals for the governor as the official selecting the judges who constitute the annexation court. In 1952 the entire statute was revised and re-enacted, conferring broader discretion on the judges of annexation courts. There have been various changes, but the utilization of the circuit court judges as outside arbiters and the general procedure employed have been unaltered throughout more than a half-century.

Initiating the Process

The process of judicial determination of annexation proposals in Virginia can be started in a number of ways.[14] A city or town can petition by passing an ordinance. The ordinance sets forth the necessity for and expediency of the proposed annexation and contains information about the boundaries of the area to be annexed, its present and future land uses, and the terms and conditions upon which the annexation is

[14] Virginia is unique in that incorporated places of 5,000 or more population that have converted from town to city status (or those of less than 5,000 that had charters before adoption of the constitution in 1902) are independent cities that do not lie within the boundaries of a county. Thus, cities in annexing take area, population and taxable values from an adjoining county. Annexations by towns do not have comparable effects because towns are located within counties. Other states considering adoption of the judicial process of annexation do not need to add the practice of city-county separation; neither is dependent on the other.

sought. Alternative methods involve petition by 51 per cent of the qualified voters of any territory adjacent to a city or town, the governing body of the county in which such area is located, or the governing body of an incorporated town wanting to be annexed. The petition states that it is desirable for such territory to be annexed and describes its boundaries.

Under all methods the interested public officials must be notified of the proposal, and the public must be informed through its publication at least once a week for four successive weeks in a newspaper issued in the city or county. The petition is sent to the circuit court of the county in which the entire territory is located or, if the area proposed for annexation is intercounty, to the circuit court of the county in which the larger part of it is situated.

There are four possible methods of beginning an annexation proceeding, but the one much the most frequently used has been initiation by a city or a town (usually the former) desiring to annex. The only other method that actually has been employed is petition by the voters of the territory. Authorizations of initial action by the governing body of the county containing the territory or by the governing body of a town desiring to be annexed were inserted into the law in 1952, but have not yet been used. Under existing legislation, however, the territory of a town—generally an incorporated place of less than 5,000 people—can be included in an annexation proposition by a city, or by another town or by the town wishing to be annexed. The sole requirement is that the proposed annexation must include all of the area of the town. Conversely, a city cannot be annexed.

Constituting the Annexation Court

After the petition is filed with the circuit court of the county, a special annexation court consisting of three circuit court judges is established. One, called the "local judge," is the judge of the circuit court of the county in which the territory under consideration is located. The other two are selected from remote circuits by the chief justice of the Supreme Court of Appeals. If the local judge disqualifies himself, all three members are chosen by the chief justice from remote circuit courts. The local judge alone hears an uncontested proceeding. Such actions are exceptional, and in most instances the special three-judge court, without jury, hears evidence in the same manner as in civil cases.

The Metropolitan Record: Annexation

Although almost always the major contention is between officials of the municipality and the county, other groups, individuals, and any adjoining city or town may become plaintiffs or defendants in the proceedings and may be represented by counsel. Prior to hearing the case the court, or at its discretion the local judge, holds a pre-trial conference with the parties that will appear, mainly to simplify the issues. In hearing the case, the court receives the evidence presented by all participants and is bound by the facts revealed.

Determining Necessity and Expediency

The annexation court must make its determinations in accordance with standards specified by the legislature. It usually is much influenced, also, by previous judicial interpretations of the legislative provisions. The major statutory guide since the original passage of the annexation law provides for the annexation courts to determine the necessity for and expediency of annexation. The courts never have stated precisely what constitutes necessity and expediency, but they have consistently considered a series of factors that are elaborations of elements mentioned by a State Supreme Court case in 1906. The court then stated that

> The necessity for or expediency of enlargements [of municipal boundaries] is determined by the health of the community, its size, its crowded conditions, its past growth, and the need in the reasonably near future for [its] development and expansion. These are matters of fact, and when they so exist as to satisfy the judicial mind of the necessity for or expediency of annexation, then, in accordance with the provisions of the act, the same must be declared.[15]

In determining whether or not a proposed annexation is necessary and expedient, the annexation court considers four factors that are in large part outgrowths of this opinion of 1906. Any one of them may be decisive, but ordinarily a composite of them forms the basis of the decision, made after a balanced consideration of all the interests affected by the case. A municipality seeking to annex advances evidence in support of these four factors while the county and others in opposition try to prove that the testimony is insufficient or erroneous.

Generally, the first factor considered by the court is the municipality's need for additional territory in order to grow and develop. The

---

[15] *Henrico County* v. *City of Richmond*, 106 Va. 294–295 (1906). In 1928 the state annexation law of 1904 was amended to require the annexation courts to determine necessity *and* expediency.

necessity for added area may be indicated in terms of congested conditions or lack of suitable land for residential and industrial building sites within the present municipal borders. Population and land use data usually are presented, the former to indicate that the municipality's area is becoming more populous and more densely settled, the latter to demonstrate its sparsity of usable vacant land. The second factor considered is the need for governmental services in the area to be annexed. Information is furnished on service deficiencies in it and the kinds and levels of services that the municipality can provide compared with those currently supplied by the county.

The third factor is the existence of a community of interests between the municipality and the territory proposed to be annexed. Here consideration is given to the degree to which close social, economic and cultural relationships are present. The fourth issue is the annexing municipality's financial ability to discharge the obligations that will grow out of the annexation. In this connection an analysis is presented of the present financial condition of the annexing government and the effect of the proposal on its finances.

After the hearing, the annexation court must decide from the evidence submitted and its personal observation of the territory whether to approve or deny the proposed annexation. If a majority of the judges is not convinced of the necessity and expediency of the proposition, the petition is dismissed. A denial similarly is made if the court finds that the municipality has annexed territory from the same county during the previous five years. The petition also is dismissed if the city or town has not complied substantially with the conditions of its immediately preceding annexation, unless compliance was impossible or insufficient time had passed. Conversely, if the court majority is satisfied that the annexation is necessary and expedient, it is mandatory for the court to determine the terms and conditions of the annexation and to enter an order granting the petition.

Fixing the Boundaries

Before setting the terms and conditions of annexation, the court must determine the boundaries of the area to be annexed. It may include a larger or a smaller amount of territory than that described in the petition. In most instances the court has not altered the proposed limits, but the existence of the authority to do so serves as a safeguard against cities and towns seeking only land with high taxable resources. The judicial determination of boundaries must adhere to certain legislative requirements relating to local governments operating in the area. Thus, although an entire town can be absorbed, neither a city nor a part of a town can be annexed. When only part of a county is annexed, the annexation cannot reduce the remaining county to less than sixty square miles or to what are deemed insufficient population or revenue sources.[16]

Legislative requirements of a different nature also must be followed by the annexation court. One provides that the lines of annexation must be drawn so as to include a reasonably compact body of land. However, areas separated from each other can be annexed in the same proceeding if each is contiguous to the annexing municipality. Two other stipulations are related to this standard of reasonable compactness. They are not effective if certain lands which they otherwise would exclude must be embraced to provide a compact area. One of these stipulations prohibits inclusion of land that is not adapted to municipal improvements; this has been interpreted to refer to the physical characteristics of the land rather than its present use. The other requirement forbids inclusion of land that is not needed by the municipality for its development in the reasonably near future; this has prevented cities and towns from absorbing large amounts of rural territory currently in use for agricultural purposes.

Setting the Terms and Conditions

The annexation court has authority to establish several kinds of terms and conditions. It requires the annexing city or town to assume a just proportion of the existing debt of the county or of affected special districts within the county. It decides on the amount to be paid by the city or town for the value of public improvements transferred from the county. Furthermore, since cities do not lie within counties in Virginia, an annexing city (or town if it becomes a city within the subsequent five years) can be ordered to compensate the county for its prospective loss of net tax revenues during the next five years. However, in place of such compensation, the court can provide for retention of any public improvements by the county, or for joint county-city or county-town use of them under judicially imposed conditions. It also prescribes the

[16] These provisions on size and resources of counties result from utilization of city-county separation in Virginia and do not apply in other states.

capital outlays and capital improvements to be made by the city in the area after annexation to satisfy the needs of the residents and to bring the facilities up to the standard maintained in other parts of the city. Ordinarily the affected parties are permitted to work out mutually satisfactory terms, which are then incorporated in the judicial order. The court makes the determinations only when agreement cannot be reached.

The Rights to Decline and Appeal

Before entry of the annexation order, the council of the city or town, upon approval of the court, can decline to accept the annexation on the terms and conditions specified. Under these circumstances the municipality has to pay its own court costs and those of the county. In addition, it cannot seek to annex territory in the same county in the ensuing five years. This provision was inserted in 1952, and no city or town has yet declined the annexation. An appeal from the annexation court's decision may be made to the Virginia Supreme Court of Appeals by the city, the town or any parties in the suit, and the Supreme Court can uphold, reverse or modify the judgment. Most requests for review are granted, but for more than a half-century surprisingly few have been made.

The annexation court remains in existence for five years from the effective date of its order or from the time of the Supreme Court's decision affirming the order. During this period, the annexation court may reconvene by its own action, a motion of the governing body of one of the affected governments, or a petition of fifty voters in the annexed area. The purpose of reconvening is to enforce performance of the terms and conditions of annexation. Added to the annexation law in the statutory revision of 1952, this option so far has been unused. The actions of the reconvened court are subject to review by the Supreme Court.

The Importance of the Judicial Procedure

The judicial annexation process has proved to be highly significant in Virginia. Its most basic importance is that it provides a method for the orderly growth and development of municipalities through absorption of adjacent territory. The record of annexations by cities—and cities rather than towns have been involved in most actions—is impressive.

The Metropolitan Record: Annexation

In the period from 1904 through 1954 cities annexed a total of 201 square miles, including the areas of nine towns. Five of the metropolitan central cities—Newport News, Norfolk, Portsmouth, Richmond and Roanoke—acquired 54 per cent of all territory annexed by Virginia cities.[17] Boundary extensions were granted in almost 95 per cent of all proceedings heard on their merits, although in about one-third of the court orders cities received less than they proposed. The annexations ranged from a fraction of a square mile to approximately twenty-eight square miles.

The annexation procedure in Virginia has eliminated unsound, capricious and selective annexations, which sometimes occur elsewhere. Municipalities have had to undertake thorough studies before instituting annexation suits. The necessity of justifying the annexation proposal before the special court has precluded hasty, ill-considered actions. In addition, cities and towns have been compelled to annex land that is urban. Thus they have been unable to annex agriculturally productive land or to avoid including territory with low financial resources.

Under the judicial determination procedure the decision on proposed annexations is the responsibility of an independent, impartial group that can balance the community-wide needs and the individual interests of all parties involved. The arbiters are skilled at distinguishing the essential from the trivial, and the proceedings are conducted under well-established procedural rules in a dignified atmosphere. Evidence is heard on its merits, and judgments are rendered without favoritism.

Extensive Approval

The annexation procedure in Virginia has received wide support in the state and has been acclaimed repeatedly by observers elsewhere. On three occasions the Virginia Legislature has had official studies made of the annexation law, the first two in 1940 and 1942 by the Virginia Advisory Legislative Council, the most recent in 1951 by a specially constituted Commission to Study Urban Growth. All except the initial report suggested some changes, but each recommended against altering the basic features of the statute and strongly supported judicial determination of annexation. For example, the 1951 commission concluded:

---

[17] The individual totals are Newport News, 2.17 square miles; Norfolk, 42.7; Portsmouth, 9.44; Richmond, 33.61; and Roanoke, 20.7. Hampton and Warwick, the two other metropolitan central cities in the state, incorporated in 1952 and have not annexed.

On the question of deciding the case on a political or judicial basis the Commission is emphatically opposed to any change because no abuse has been shown and the court is skilled in deciding the merits of opposing claims. No other agency is as impartial as the courts.

. . . .

The Commission considered at length the question of holding an election in annexation cases. This consideration extended to an election in (a) the area to be annexed, (b) the annexing city or town, (c) the county from which the territory is to be annexed, and (d) various combinations of the foregoing. Many bills have been introduced in the General Assembly on this subject. After mature deliberation the Commission decided against recommending an election in annexation either on an advisory or binding basis. The reasons for this are: annexation should depend upon the facts of each case as it is a legal and economic question. The problem of placing citizens with common interests under a common government will not be solved by an election. If the election is advisory only and the court decides adversely ill feeling will be aggravated. In brief, the merits of annexation will not be considered in an election.[18]

Recommendation for an Administrative Tribunal

Persons in the state who oppose decisions on annexation at the polls, however, are not unanimous in favoring judicial decision. One advocate of modifying the present procedure is Chester W. Bain of the University of Virginia, who recently completed the first comprehensive analysis of the Virginia annexation practice. He objects strongly to voter decision on annexation propositions. In view of the issues and the nature of the decisions in annexation actions before the courts during the last half century, he observes, it would be unwise to vest control of such questions in an affected city or town, fringe, or county.[19]

Although supporting non-voter determination of annexation questions, Professor Bain concludes that the current judicial process has certain deficiencies. The special annexation courts, he holds, are temporary agencies that do not accumulate and use a sustained body of information and knowledge about annexation matters. The procedure is cumbersome and expensive. He raises serious doubt as to whether the issues involve decisions of a legal nature and concludes that "it is hard to accept the judgment that these are types of judicial determinations that courts of law are normally called upon to make."[20] A major

[18] Virginia Commission to Study Urban Growth, *Report* (Richmond: 1951), pp. 5, 6.

[19] Chester W. Bain, "Annexation in Virginia: The Use of the Judicial Process for Readjusting City-County Boundaries" (Charlottesville: University of Virginia Bureau of Public Administration, 1955, typewritten manuscript), p. 390. A major portion of this able study, which has been useful in preparing the present analysis of Virginia annexation, will be published soon.

[20] *Ibid.*, p. 402.

recommendation in Professor Bain's study is to replace the annexation court composed of circuit judges with a state administrative agency or tribunal possessing quasi-judicial powers, whose findings on annexation matters would be final except on questions of law.

The suggestion is similar to one by an out-of-state analyst who considers it questionable whether, in some states, the Virginia procedure would be judged to be a constitutional delegation of legislative power to the judiciary.[21] He concludes, however, that basically the same approach is possible without utilizing the judiciary. The same result can be achieved and the possible constitutional barrier of improper delegation avoided by establishment of an administrative tribunal at the state level, charged with making determinations on annexation proposals.

It might be advisable in some states to grant such an administrative tribunal additional authority to make judgments about incorporations, because at times there is a close relationship between annexation and incorporation in fringe area situations. Some states have very low minimum requirements for incorporation, under which urban developments without adequate financial resources are able to establish separate, formal existences. Although in a legal sense they convert from an unincorporated to an incorporated status (and thus generally gain immunity from being annexed), they remain substandard members of the urban community in terms of services and regulation. They are still fringe problems. Endowing a state administrative agency handling annexation matters with power to determine the feasibility of proposed incorporations in urban fringes, and with authority to order the annexation of small substandard areas that have incorporated previously, could avoid such circumstances.

Implementation of the Laws

More than improved legislation is needed if annexation is to be an effective device in solving urban fringe area difficulties. Regardless of the annexation method adopted in individual states, cities must assume leadership by formulating and using intelligent annexation programs. Although the fringe problem is intergovernmental, its most direct and continuing effects are on municipalities. Unless an annexation court or

---

[21] Robert E. Fryer, *Analysis of Annexation in Michigan Together With a Comparison of Annexation in Other States* (Ann Arbor: University of Michigan Bureau of Government, 1951), p. 47.

administrative tribunal exists to apply standards in annexation efforts, cities should adopt at least four policy guides as major parts of their programs. Annexations should be general—not selective on the basis of favorable conditions and lucrative financial resources in the fringe. They should be undertaken prior to heavy urbanization of the fringe, so that proper controls can be initiated before inferior developments materialize, which are costly to rectify. Annexations should conform to principles of sound financing, so that when areas are absorbed a full complement of municipal services can be provided in a reasonable period of time without severe dislocation of the city's finances. Annexations should meet the standard of well-balanced, over-all city development, which calls for improvements in both the new and older city sectors rather than concentration on one area at the expense of the others.

Studying the Fringe

Sound municipal annexation programs must consist of study, distribution of information and action. To be informed adequately and to act wisely, the city must collect and evaluate various types of facts. It must acquire a thorough understanding of the fringe. This involves assembling and analyzing data about the people of the fringe, its social and economic characteristics, its existing improvements and developments, and the nature and direction of its growth. The city must fully understand its current relationships with the fringe and the present and probably future effects of the fringe on the city. It must appraise the costs of annexation and its financial ability to meet them. It must determine its capacity to provide the services needed in the fringe. Nashville, Louisville and Norfolk are illustrations of metropolitan central cities where such studies have been undertaken in recent years. Especially noteworthy is *A Future for Nashville*, prepared in 1951 by the Community Services Commission for Davidson County and the City of Nashville.

Distributing Information

Supplying information on the effects and benefits of annexation is a significant element in a municipal annexation program. This is an obvious requirement when fringe inhabitants have the right to vote on the annexation proposal. It is less apparent but equally important for developing good will among these future city dwellers and voters even if they cannot vote on annexation. An example of an extensive information program was that undertaken by San Antonio in its non-voting fringe prior to the city's large-scale annexation of 1952. The residents of the city as well as those of the fringe need to be informed. Only by disseminating the facts to the people of both fringe and city can misinformation be counteracted successfully and misunderstanding eliminated.

In recent years Milwaukee and Sacramento, among other cities, have had outstanding information programs. In *Annexation: Key to Prosperous Community*, Milwaukee explains through its department of community development how the annexation of territory contributes substantially to solution of numerous area problems. The educational bulletins of Sacramento's planning staff demonstrate the advantages of obtaining more and improved municipal services. They also indicate the practicality of immediate and long-range planning and other mutual benefits of annexation to the fringe and the city.

In various communities, newspaper accounts, public meetings, radio, television, house-to-house contacts, and citizen committees have been important in the information programs. Some cities carry their programs over into the post-annexation period. They distribute booklets to residents of newly annexed areas, welcoming them as citizens and explaining important services that are now available. Prominent examples are *A Message of Welcome from Your City Government*, issued by Kansas City, Missouri; *Life in San Jose, California;* and Oklahoma City's *This Is Your City*.

Action

Having studied all foreseeable aspects of annexing the fringe, the city government is in an excellent position for action. It will not be confronted unexpectedly and disadvantageously by an annexation proposal from another quarter. The city cannot always choose the time when annexation action will start, for others possess the right to initiate it, and will probably continue to have it. But, unlike the widespread situation today, the city will have the facts at hand to benefit from the action, if it is sound, whatever its originating source. If the city itself intends to initiate annexation, however, it must guard against a common current mistake—deferring too long.

Improved annexation laws and their intelligent use can be important steps in metropolitan progress. Usually they will not solve the metropolitan problem, because they operate within a relatively narrow geographical framework created by prohibitions against absorbing incorporated places. Despite this limitation they can make significant contributions. Annexations can alleviate the urban fringe difficulty, which is ordinarily part of the metropolitan problem. They can serve as a supplement to, and in some instances as a substitute for, other approaches aimed at rectifying the governmental shortcomings of metropolitan areas.

The metropolitan significance of annexation sometimes has been underrated, at times overvalued. The basic needs are to strengthen the device and to realize both its potentialities and its limitations.

2. CITY–COUNTY CONSOLIDATION

City-county consolidation has received consideration in many parts of the United States as one approach in dealing with the metropolitan problem. It usually takes one of three forms. The most extensive is the complete merger of the governments of the county and the municipalities within it into a single government. A second consists of the substantial merger of these units, but retention of the county government—ordinarily for limited purposes—as a separate legal identity. A third involves unification of some of the municipal governments and the county government. Occasionally these forms of city-county consolidation are broadened to encompass the territory of two or more counties and the county and municipal governments within them, or to include other local governments, or both.

Despite widespread advocacy, city-county consolidation seldom has been adopted. In only five places—New Orleans, Boston, Philadelphia, New York and Baton Rouge—has it gone into effect in the major part or all of an area that was then or later became metropolitan. Each merits individual consideration of its principal characteristics.[1]

The New Orleans Consolidation

In 1805, two years after the United States completed the purchase of the Louisiana Territory, the first session of the territorial legislature laid out the same boundaries for the City of New Orleans and the Parish (County) of Orleans. The first state constitution of Louisiana was adopted in 1812. In the next year a state law authorized the governmental authorities of the City of New Orleans to perform within the city boundaries the legislative and administrative functions assigned by law to the police jury (governing body) of each parish. The same legislation specifically prohibited the police jury of the Parish of Orleans from exercising such powers within the city. This state action thus resulted in the consolidation of some activities of two formerly separate, but coterminous, governmental units.

---

[1] City-county separation and federation (the borough plan) differ sufficiently from city-county consolidation to warrant separate treatment. When effected in 1952 the only other city-county consolidation—the Hampton area of Virginia (see page 83)—did not include the major portion of a metropolitan area.

Changes Through State Legislation

Three types of state legislative acts that affected the consolidation were instituted subsequently during the nineteenth century. Each of them proved to be temporary in its entirety or in large part. One was the re-establishment in 1822 of the independent governing body of the Parish of Orleans. During most of its quarter century of existence thereafter, until 1846, it had only limited powers, principally that of general taxation. A second alteration, effective from 1836 to 1852, was division of the City of New Orleans into three municipalities or districts. Another development, initiated earlier, was a series of detachments of territory from the city and the parish. The largest of the detachments resulted in the creation of Jefferson Parish, which still exists and contains more than double the area remaining in the city and parish of which it had been a part. These separations began shortly after the partial city-parish consolidation had been completed in 1813, and they decreased the size of the area to which the consolidation applied. By 1874 many of the separated areas had been reabsorbed into the city and, as a consequence, automatically into the parish. Neither the city nor the parish has been subjected to later realignment of boundaries.

The original, basic pattern of consolidation has continued in later years without further modifications. Most local governmental activities are carried out on a parish-wide basis by agencies of the city government. However, numerous officers of the parish—such as two sheriffs who serve primarily as aides to the courts in criminal and civil proceedings, the district attorney, the coroner, the recorder of mortgages, the recorder of conveyances, various court clerks and the judges of parish courts of general jurisdiction—are independently elected. Their elective status is guaranteed by provisions in the state constitution. Although the voters of the parish and of the city are the same, these officers are not formal parts of the consolidated government, and the latter has no power or control over them. In addition, public school affairs are handled by an independent school district.

The Boston Consolidation

For more than a century and a half county governmental affairs in Suffolk County, which includes Boston, were the responsibility of the justices of the court of sessions. This arrangement, inaugurated in 1643

The Metropolitan Record: Consolidation

when the colonial legislature initially established shires or counties, terminated through action of the state legislature in 1821. The change was prompted by considerable controversy over taxation and highway matters between the court and the governing body of the Town of Boston.

The legislation of 1821 transferred the judicial functions of the court of sessions to other courts and allotted its remaining powers to the aldermen (one house of the city council) and the mayor of Boston. The law became effective in 1822, the same year in which Boston became the first Massachusetts community to convert from town to city status. Subsequent creation of county commissioners on a state-wide basis, in 1827, did not modify the existing arrangement in Suffolk County. The mayor of Boston exercises the executive powers vested in county commissioners elsewhere in the state, and the city council possesses the legislative powers in Suffolk County.

Special Position of Three Cities and Towns

Under the consolidation act, the City of Boston gained title to most county property and assumed the expenses of the county government. Also, the duties of the county treasurer were assigned to the city treasurer. In 1879 the county auditing functions were transferred to the city auditor.

When the consolidation law of 1821 was adopted, the limits of Boston had not been extended, and the county contained not only Boston but also the Town (later City) of Chelsea, which had been separated from Boston in 1739. In 1852 and 1871 two sections split off from Chelsea. Consequently, there now exist in Suffolk County three cities—Boston, Chelsea and Revere—and one town, Winthrop.

The people of Chelsea, Revere and Winthrop benefit from the services and facilities of the county government and participate in the election of county officers not part of the consolidated government. They do not pay any of the county costs, which totaled more than $6.5 million in 1955; all county costs are paid by Boston. Under a state law of 1831 Boston acquired full title to all county property, while Chelsea gave up its title to county property and was exempted from taxes for county purposes. The tax exemption has been applicable also to Revere and Winthrop, because they were parts of Chelsea when the act was passed. The law gave Chelsea the privilege of applying to the legislature at any time after twenty years for withdrawal from Suffolk County and inclusion in another county, but the privilege has not been used.

The financial arrangement just described has received increased criticism as the two cities and the town outside Boston have grown in population and assessed valuation. Nevertheless, neither the repeated efforts of Boston's legislative representatives nor recommendations of other official groups, such as a special commission appointed by the governor in 1913, have prevailed in the state legislature.[2]

Combined Operations

The combined city and county responsibilities of the city council, mayor, treasurer, and auditor enable the city government of Boston to perform a number of county activities. The penal institutions department, under the city government, administers the county house of corrections and exercises the power to parole prisoners committed there and to the county jail. The city is responsible for the maintenance and operation of certain county buildings, and the mayor appoints the head of the county buildings department. City officials handle the financial administration of county offices, including budgeting, auditing, tax collection, custody of funds and some purchasing. The debts of the county constitute city indebtedness.

Suffolk County retains its legal identity principally because it is a governmental area for the administration of justice, for criminal prosecutions and for keeping certain public records. A considerable part of the executive authority in the county is scattered among numerous officials who are elected independently or are appointed by the state government. The county officers elected by the county voters are the district attorney, the register of probate, the register of deeds, the clerk of the criminal session and the clerk of the civil session of the superior court, and the sheriff, who aids the courts and manages the county jail. Two types of additional county officials—the index commissioner, responsible for consolidating indexes in the registry of deeds, and two medical examiners—are appointed by the governor. Judges serving in local jurisdictions are selected by the governor with the consent of his executive council.

[2] Recent views on the situation and suggested alternatives are contained in Boston Finance Commission, *Report . . . on the Executive Branch of the (Boston) City Government* (Boston: 1950), pp. 54–57. The finance commission consists of appointees of the governor. In 1956 the upper house of the Massachusetts legislature passed a bill to have Chelsea, Revere and Winthrop share in paying the county costs.

The Philadelphia Consolidation

Initial State Legislative Actions

Recognition of lax law enforcement, which was very apparent at the time of a series of riots, served as the motivating force that led to city-county consolidation in the Philadelphia area. A citizens' committee, formed in 1849 and representative of all Philadelphia County, obtained passage of a state law in 1850 establishing a unified police system for the city and other sections of the county. Convinced of the benefits of this functional merger, the committee continued its work for local governmental reform, and it emphasized the general inability of the many local units to meet various county-wide problems.

In 1854, after the citizens' group succeeded in a local campaign to elect state legislators pledged to major consolidation, the legislature responded by enacting a comprehensive consolidation act. The boundaries of the City of Philadelphia were made identical with those of the County of Philadelphia. Twenty-eight local governments in the county, consisting of boroughs, townships and other units, were combined with the city government under the name "City of Philadelphia."

The county government was modified but not eliminated. Its two governing bodies (a regular board of county commissioners, and another board which consisted of the county's state senators and which reviewed specific important actions of the other) were abolished, and their legislative functions were reassigned to the city council, then a bicameral body. The county treasurer and the county auditor were supplanted by the city treasurer and the city controller. Under the control of the city council, three newly established city commissioners assumed the administrative duties of the abolished county commissioners concerning such matters as assessments, elections and jury selection. Title to all county property was given over to the city, which assumed the debt of all governments involved in the consolidation. Public education, previously a county function, also was affected; the consolidation act included the school district as a department of the city government.[3]

While requiring the merging of numerous governments, the combining and supplanting of various offices, and the reallocating of public property and debt, the consolidation act also stipulated that the county

[3] Through other laws the school district was endowed with considerable autonomy in managing school affairs but continued to come under the appropriation power of the consolidated government. In 1911 the district gained complete independence and the power to levy its own taxes.

was to continue in existence. All county officers not abolished by the legislation were to continue to be elected in accordance with existing laws and constitutional provisions. Thus the following county officers continued to be elected: the district attorney, the sheriff (primarily a judicial administrative officer), the coroner, the recorder of deeds, the recorder of wills, the clerk of the court of quarter sessions (serving the courts in criminal matters), and the prothonotary (serving the courts in civil matters). But, although they continued to be elective county officers, the city council assumed control of their finances.[4] Local judges, regarded as state judicial officers, were not included in the consolidation. The net result of the consolidation act of 1854, however, was that most of the total responsibility for local government within the County of Philadelphia rested directly or indirectly on the consolidated city government of Philadelphia.

The New State Constitution and Court Decisions

The original degree of consolidation was lessened by provisions contained in the new state constitution of 1874 and by court interpretations of them within the following two decades. The three city commissioners, the city treasurer and the city controller became county officers, the first three through a section in the new constitution and the latter two by subsequent decisions of the State Supreme Court. These five, together with all county officers not abolished by the consolidation act of 1854, received constitutional status as elective officials, except for the prothonotary of Philadelphia County, who became the appointee of the local common pleas judges. Designation of these posts in the state constitution safeguarded them from later state legislation abolishing or merging the offices with other offices or making the officeholders appointees of the consolidated city government.

The state legislature was vested with broad authority over county officers. It determined their compensation and the extent of their duties; it established—or permitted particular county officers to establish—the number and compensation of subordinate employees. Although Philadelphia's city government remained the tax-levying and appropriating body, its actual control over county budget requests had become limited. The extent of the original consolidation had been diminished through increase of the independence of county officials by placing them in the constitution and through enlargement of their total number.

[4] Studenski, *The Government of Metropolitan Areas in the United States*, pp. 193–194.

Efforts to Obtain a Constitutional Amendment

Not until the 1930's did a relatively concerted effort get under way to make the consolidation complete. The need for obtaining legislative and voter acceptance of a state constitutional change represented a large hurdle to be overcome. In 1935, four years after a similar proposal had been introduced unsuccessfully, the legislature adopted a joint resolution for a constitutional amendment. It proposed that "the County of Philadelphia as distinct from the City of Philadelphia be abolished, and that all county functions be devolved upon the officers of the city." The state constitution requires that such resolutions be passed in two successive legislative sessions before an amendment can be submitted to popular vote. The resolution of 1935 was adopted by the legislature again at its next session, in 1937. Later in the same year the electorate defeated it; the proposal received a 47 per cent affirmative vote. Residents of Philadelphia County voted in favor, three to two, but the electorate in the rest of the state recorded a negative plurality that was decisive. Similar resolutions failed in the legislature in 1945 and 1947. But the legislature passed a comparable measure in 1949 and again in 1951, and in late 1951 the voters overwhelmingly approved the constitutional amendment. It received more than a ten-to-one majority in Philadelphia County and a three-to-one margin throughout the state.

In 1951, several months before voter approval of the amendment, a new city charter was adopted in Philadelphia. It contained a section granting the city council the fullest authority consistent with the consolidation amendment and with a state legislative act of 1949 that conferred the charter-making power on Philadelphia. Two schools of thought regarding this charter section quickly grew up. One held that it could become operative only if the legislature enacted enabling legislation after adoption of the consolidation amendment. The other felt that upon passage of the amendment the section could be put into effect by the city acting alone.[5]

A State Enabling Law

Because of this difference of opinion, the city's advisory commission on consolidation suggested that the legislature specifically authorize the city council to act. Meanwhile, the State Supreme Court ruled that two county officers, the elected register of wills and the appointed prothono-

[5] Bureau of Municipal Research of Philadelphia, *The Problem of Completing City-County Consolidation* (Philadelphia: 1952), p. 5.

tary, were judicial officers to whom the consolidation amendment did not apply because of other provisions in the constitution. In 1953 the legislature passed a law authorizing city council action with respect to five county offices. In line with the authorization, the council subsequently converted the city treasurer, coroner and recorder of deeds from elected officials to appointees of the city government; it also made an independent office, the board of inspectors of the Philadelphia County prison, a part of a city department. Another section of the state act specified that certain officials and agencies, including the sheriff and the city commissioners, were to continue in all respects as they were before adoption of the 1951 constitutional amendment. This in effect exempted them from the personnel, fiscal and other management controls of the consolidated city government—but the section was declared unconstitutional in 1954 by the State Supreme Court.

Court Decision on Independent City Action

The city council then decided to act on its own. Less than five months after the judicial action of 1954, the council passed an ordinance abolishing the county tax revision board and transferring its functions elsewhere in the city government. In early 1955 the Pennsylvania Supreme Court declared the ordinance invalid on the basis of the wording of a section of the constitutional amendment. The court noted that the section states "... all (former) county officers shall continue (as city officers) to perform their duties and be elected (or) appointed, compensated and organized as may be provided by ... existing laws *until the General Assembly shall otherwise provide.*" (The parenthetical material and italics were added by the court.) The court reasoned that this section of the constitutional amendment certainly superseded the right of the city council to act independently, even if it were assumed that prior to the amendment's adoption the council might have been permitted to do so by the legislative act conferring the charter-making power on Philadelphia and the charter based on that act. The court concluded that the ordinance was unconstitutional since the state legislature had not vested in the city the power that the city council had attempted to use.

The intent of the consolidation amendment thus was settled by court interpretation more than three years after its approval by the people. The amendment was intended to transform county offices into Philadelphia city offices, but any actual alteration in these offices could be accomplished only if the legislature reorganized them or authorized the city to do so.[6]

City-county consolidation in Philadelphia has advanced since 1951 after an interlude of inaction spanning many decades. All county employees have been included in the city's merit system, and all county officials and agencies have been brought under the fiscal and other housekeeping controls that operate throughout the consolidated city government. However, only one-third of the twelve independent county offices and agencies that existed at the time of the constitutional amendment have actually been integrated into the consolidated organization. Future developments depend upon the state legislature passing reorganization laws of its own or enabling legislation under which the consolidated city government can act.

The New York Consolidation

The First Consolidations

City-county consolidation has been used three times in the New York area, but the plan that went into operation in 1898 is the best known, and it involved the largest amount of territory. The first consolidation occurred in the colonial period. In 1730, under a new city charter granted by the colonial governor, the boundaries of the County of New York and the City of New York were made identical, and the city board of aldermen assumed the functions of the county board of supervisors. The other county officers were not affected. Through state legislative action in 1894 a similar but broader development took place in another part of the area. The boundaries of the City of Brooklyn and the County of Kings were made coterminous. The powers of the county supervisor-at-large, the board of county supervisors and the county auditor were transferred to the mayor, the city council and the city auditor, respectively, and the duties of the city treasurer were given over to the county treasurer. Thus two local precedents existed for the larger and more comprehensive consolidation that became effective in 1898 in a metropolitan area of more than three million people.

[6] The intricate sequence of events pertaining to consolidation since 1951 is presented in Bureau of Municipal Research of Philadelphia, "Taking Stock of Consolidation," *Citizens' Business*, No. 2072S, December 21, 1953, and Bureau of Municipal Research of Philadelphia and Pennsylvania Economy League, Eastern Division, "Supreme Court Delays Completing City-County Unity," *Citizens' Business*, No. 2095, January 24, 1955.

The Consolidation of 1898

In 1894, the same year in which the Brooklyn-Kings County consolidation law was passed, the legislature enacted a measure providing for an over-all popular vote on the question of consolidating the local governments in an area covering the three counties of New York, Kings and Richmond, and part of a fourth, Queens. The vote was to be advisory only, not binding on the legislature. Some communities, including Brooklyn and Flushing, recorded small negative margins, but these were overcome by the affirmative vote elsewhere. A large total majority favored the idea.

Less than two years later, in 1896, the legislature passed a consolidation act for the area. It provided for appointment by the governor of a commission to prepare a charter for the consolidated government and for continuance of the existing local governments pending approval of the charter. The state legislation was subject to veto by the mayor of any city in the consolidated area, and the mayors of New York and Brooklyn proceeded to exercise the right. The legislature then repassed the law over their vetoes.

The legislation imposed two restrictions on the scope of the charter commission's activities. One was that an equal and uniform rate of taxation should be provided throughout the consolidated territory. The second, although liberally interpreted by the charter drafters, made certain that the consolidation, at least at its inauguration, would be partial in nature. It stipulated that the charter was not to affect the boundaries and the governments of the counties. The completed charter was approved by the legislature in 1897, after it had made minor alterations. The mayor of New York vetoed the charter and the legislature repassed it. The charter became effective on January 1, 1898.

Territorial and Functional Changes

The consolidation was comprehensive in many ways. The limits of the City of New York were extended to encompass the territory of four (and subsequently five) counties.[7] The counties continued to exist within the consolidated area, but a large share of the administrative and

---

[7] The portion of Queens County not included in the consolidation was made into the County of Nassau in 1898, and fourteen years later the County of New York, which was part of the consolidated area, was divided, resulting in the formation of the County of the Bronx.

The Metropolitan Record: Consolidation

legislative responsibilities of their governments was reallocated to the city government. For example, the existing boards of county supervisors were abolished; all elective county offices not specified in the state constitution were eliminated and their duties transferred to their city government counterparts. However, the merger of county operations with those of the city could not be complete because the state constitution required the separate existence of certain county posts. The major offices excluded from the consolidation initially were the elective positions of county judge, county clerk, district attorney and sheriff, in each county.[8]

The Boroughs

The New York plan is unique among completed city-county consolidations in granting to local areas, called boroughs, both specific local administrative powers and direct participation on a major policy agency of the consolidated government.[9] The five boroughs of Manhattan, Brooklyn, Bronx, Queens and Richmond were created; each has been coterminous with a county since the County of the Bronx was formed in 1912. The residents of each borough elect a borough president, who is its administrative head, responsible for discharging functions assigned in the charter to the boroughs. Under the original charter, in addition to performing certain specified local duties, a borough president was a member of two types of boards. He served on local improvement boards that made recommendations to the city government on proposed public works in the borough to be financed entirely or partly by local special assessments. He also served on the city board of public improvements, which was concerned with proposals regarding water supply, highways, street cleaning, sewers, public buildings and lighting, and bridges. However, on the latter board—which had to report favor-

---

[8] Under a constitutional amendment initiated in the 1934–35 legislative sessions, and subsequently approved by the voters, New York City was empowered to abolish any county offices other than those of judges, county clerks and district attorneys and to reassign the functions of the abolished offices. Provision was made for appointment of the county clerks by the appellate division of the State Supreme Court. The amendment also prohibited enactment of state legislation relating to county matters in the City of New York, except by means of an emergency message of the governor and concurrent action by two-thirds vote of both legislative houses. A mayor-appointed sheriff replaced the county sheriffs, and the posts of registrar (or register) of deeds were abolished in 1941 by city charter amendments.

[9] The boroughs, however, have no legislative powers over local matters. If they did, New York would be an example of federation and would be discussed in a later section. See page 86, footnote 2.

ably on a matter before it received consideration by the city council—a borough president could participate in the discussion, but could not vote unless the proposition affected his borough alone.

The responsibilities of borough presidents subsequently have been altered through charter changes, some of the most important of which developed in a general charter revision of 1901 and in the new charter adopted in 1937. For example, in 1901 the city board of public improvements was abolished, the board of estimates—which exercises a large share of the legislative power of the city government—was reorganized, and the five borough presidents were made members of it. In 1937 the administrative duties of the borough presidents were reduced by transferring some of their functions to the city departments of housing, building and public works and to the city board of standards and appeals.

Each borough president still possesses certain administrative powers within the borough. He appoints a commissioner of public works who is responsible for the construction of streets, small sewers, public baths and comfort stations. The borough president serves as a member of local improvement boards, which hear petitions and start proceedings on local improvements. He selects the members of local school boards and of an advisory planning board who make suggestions to the city board of education and city planning commission, respectively. The board of estimate, of which each borough president is a member, is a very important part of the city government. It determines city policy on all financial affairs, local assessments, franchises, city planning, public improvements, privileges, permits and zoning, and it has concurring power with the city council in particular types of legislation. In the board's decisions the borough president of Brooklyn has two votes, as does the borough president of Manhattan; the borough presidents of the Bronx, Richmond and Queens have one each. Together, they have seven of the total of sixteen votes, as the three city-wide officials—the mayor, the comptroller and the president of the city council—hold three votes each.

The Inclusion of Public Education

The consolidation brought increased and later complete unification of educational activities. The numerous separate school operations of the area were merged. Under the charter of 1898 school matters were divided between a city-wide board of education and four borough school boards, one of which covered the two boroughs of Manhattan and the Bronx. Each borough board, its members appointed by the mayor, determined the educational policies of schools located within the respective boroughs. The city board of education, composed of nineteen members selected from the borough boards, exercised school plant and business functions. This division of control over school affairs was eliminated in the charter revision of 1901. It reassigned the powers of the borough boards to the city board of education, which was reconstituted to contain forty-six members chosen by the mayor. That number later was reduced to seven and subsequently raised to nine. The city board assumed general authority and responsibility over the public school system.

In summary, the New York consolidation has several prominent features. The functions of many formerly independent governments are unified under one government, the City of New York, whose territory encompasses five counties. Local areas, retained and reconstituted under the name of boroughs, perform several local administrative functions and are represented on an important city-wide policy body. As a result of actions taken under the original consolidation and the constitutional amendment of the 1930's, the five county governments are largely consolidated with the city government. The district attorney, the county clerk and the public administrator, however, remain outside the jurisdiction of the consolidated government, and a separate set of these three county officials functions in each of the five counties. Relatively few types of county officials are independent, but each type is present five times.

The Baton Rouge Consolidation

The present century almost reached the midway point before its first city-county consolidation materialized. In 1945 the portions of East Baton Rouge Parish (County) that lay near the City of Baton Rouge, Louisiana, were in the midst of extensive industrial and residential development. Of the residential fringe areas, which contained approximately twice the population of the city, many were substandard in construction and lacking in urban services. A newly formed parish-city planning committee hired a professional planning firm, but it soon became evident that planning could not be put into operation effectively unless preceded by establishment of area-wide government. This, in turn, would have to be preceded by amendment of the state constitution.

The Enabling Constitutional Amendment

Interested citizens prepared and initiated a constitutional amendment permitting the drafting of a parish-wide plan of government. The amendment, approved at the general state election of 1946 by a margin of almost four to one, provided for an appointed commission of nine members to draw up the governmental plan in the form of a charter. Two members were to be selected by the city council of Baton Rouge, three by the parish police jury (county commissioners or supervisors), and one each by the parish school board, the Baton Rouge Chamber of Commerce, the director of the state public works department, and the president of Louisiana State University.

The Consolidation Charter

The commission had considerable latitude, with authority to merge or reorganize all or any local governments in the parish. The constitutional amendment placed only one condition upon the contents of the charter. Provision had to be made for the establishment of industrial, rural and urban areas, with the state constitutional limitation on parish taxes applying in the industrial and rural areas and that on city taxes in the urban areas. The difference in the limitations amounted to only three mills. Its required insertion in the charter, however, was important in gaining for the plan the backing of major industries.[10] The commission members had a maximum of one year in which to complete the document which, according to the terms of the constitutional amendment, had to be submitted to an over-all parish vote. The charter was adopted in 1947 by a margin of 307 votes of approximately 14,000 ballots cast. Slightly more than one-third of the electorate participated. The consolidation plan formulated in the charter, subject to change through approval of proposed amendments by the parish voters, became fully operative on January 1, 1949.

Taxing and Service Areas

The consolidation provided for division of the parish into an urban area, two industrial areas and a rural area. Uniform parish taxes are levied in all three types of areas. The city boundaries of Baton Rouge

[10] Thomas H. Reed, "Progress in Metropolitan Integration," *Public Administration Review*, 9 (Winter, 1949), p. 8. The parish and municipal limits are four and seven mills, respectively.

were extended to the limits of the urban area, which at the time of consolidation contained more than 100,000 people and thirty square miles, in comparison with a population of 35,000 and six and one-half square miles formerly possessed by the city. In the urban area, which is subject to city as well as parish taxes, the city government finances police and fire protection, garbage and refuse collection and disposal, street lighting, traffic regulation, sewers and sewerage works, and inspectional services. Compact lands adjacent to Baton Rouge and not part of an industrial area can be annexed to the urban area, thus automatically becoming part of the city, upon petition by a majority of the property owners of the lands followed by passage of a city council ordinance.

The two industrial areas, located north of the city, include the major industries and contain no residences. Services needed in these areas of a type usually furnished elsewhere by city governments are supplied by the industries at their own expense. Additional industrial areas can be created from portions of the rural area on petition of the owners of at least 90 per cent of the property value in the proposed area and action by the parish governing body. In the rural area, containing 500 square miles, none of the services financed by the city government in the urban area except police protection is supplied by the parish government. Other desired services are obtainable only through organization of special districts by the parish governing body. Highways and bridges are parish-wide charges.

Interlocking Governments

The legal identities of the City of Baton Rouge and the Parish of East Baton Rouge were preserved, in part because the exemption of homesteads in the state up to $2,000 of assessed valuation applies to parish taxes but not to city taxes. It was stipulated that the revenues and the expenditures of the city and the parish were to be kept separate. However, the two governments were interlocked in several ways. The city council was reconstituted to contain seven members, and the police jury of the parish was replaced by the parish council, consisting of the seven city councilmen and two other individuals elected from the rural area.[11] The office of mayor-president was created. Elected on a parish-

[11] The two councils hold regular meetings twice a month on the same day, one convening in the afternoon and the other in the evening. Jimmy M. Stoker, *Our City-Parish Government: A Thumbnail Sketch* (Baton Rouge: Baton Rouge Junior Chamber of Commerce, 1954), p. 22.

wide basis, he presides over both councils but has no vote, and he serves as the chief administrator of the two governments. He appoints the public works director, the personnel administrator, the finance director and the purchasing agent, all of whom serve both the city and the parish. The city and the parish share equally in the cost of operating the finance department, an arrangement that places a larger share of the cost on city residents and on property owners who pay both city and parish taxes. The mayor-president also selects the chief of police and the fire chief, who function only in the City of Baton Rouge. The attorney, the clerk and the treasurer are officials of both the city and the parish and are chosen by the parish council. A portion of the revenues obtained by the parish from the industrial areas must be allocated to the city.

A number of matters were left outside of the consolidation plan, either because of protection afforded to them by the state constitution or because of decisions of the charter commission. A town and a village in the parish with a combined population in 1950 of 2,300 continue in existence, although the consolidation charter prohibits incorporation in the parish of additional cities, towns or villages. The activities of the parish school district are unaffected. Recreation and parks are the responsibility of a special parish board created by constitutional amendment. Numerous parish officers, including the assessor, the sheriff who is both police officer and tax collector, the district attorney, the clerk of the court and the coroner, are independently elected in accordance with sections of the state constitution. The district and local judges also are elected. Public health activities are administered by a board whose members are appointed by the state health officer on recommendation of the parish council, and public welfare is a state rather than a local governmental function.

General Conclusions about Completed Consolidations

No Single Pattern

Numerous important generalizations emerge when the five consolidations now in operation are appraised together. The most basic is that there is no common pattern in the extent to which consolidated governments have been merged. Each consolidation is unique in this respect, and apparently none has been utilized as a model in any subsequent in-

The Metropolitan Record: Consolidation

stallation. Although they have similarities, the five consolidations actually represent five varying uses of a single approach to the metropolitan problem.

Generally Accomplished Through State Legislation

A state legislative act rather than consent of the local electorate has been the means of adopting all except one of the existing consolidations. A popular vote, tabulated on a county-wide basis, was the required deciding factor only in the Baton Rouge consolidation, which also is unique in that it had to be preceded by state-wide voter consent of an enabling constitutional amendment. In the New York area, where a local vote was held and the mayors of the affected cities had the right to veto the state law and the local charter on consolidation, the state legislature possessed the final, controlling voice. The local vote, although favorable and counted on an area-wide basis, was simply advisory, and the veto authority of the mayors could be, and was, overridden by the legislature.

Early Developments Involving Few Governments

Most consolidations went into effect a relatively long time ago. Only the Baton Rouge consolidation has materialized in this century. Three of the others have been functioning for more than a century, and the fourth became operative in 1898.

All except one of the consolidations in effect have occurred within the territory of a single county. The New York action concerned four and later five counties. Three consolidations each involved one city government and one county government located in a county containing very few, if any, additional general local governments. In the Philadelphia and New York areas, however, which were the most complex governmentally, numerous general local units were merged.

Coterminous Area of City and County

In a majority of the consolidations the area of the affected or remaining city was enlarged and made coterminous with the county or counties involved. Conversely, the cities of Boston and Baton Rouge each contained a relatively small portion of the county immediately following consolidation, although as a result of later annexations Boston now includes most of the county's territory.

Territorial Growth Nonexistent or Inconsequential

The three consolidations that initially extended the limits of the city to those of the county subsequently have had little, if any, territorial growth. Philadelphia, the only city that has grown in area, gained a small amount of territory in 1916 when the state legislature annexed to it a part of a township located in another county.

Reallocation of Functions to the City

In all except one of the consolidations, the governing body of the county government was abolished and its powers and responsibilities transferred to the city council, which consequently became the governing body of the consolidated government. Similarly, in these same consolidations the merger of varying numbers of functions consisted of reassigning them from county offices to city agencies. The Baton Rouge consolidation is the single exception to these two general developments. Relative to the governing body, the difference between the Baton Rouge plan and the other consolidations is simply a matter of degree. The parish (county) governing body was not eliminated but was reconstituted, and the city council was granted a controlling position. The county governing body is composed of the seven members elected to the city council and two other individuals popularly chosen from outside the city. Regarding the merger of functions, however, the difference is more substantial. Many functions formerly handled separately by the city and the county have been placed under the mayor-president who is the chief administrator of both the city and the county, elected on a county-wide basis.

Not Applicable to Certain Officials

Certain officials have commonly not been incorporated into the consolidations. Those generally excluded are the judges, various aides to the courts, the district attorneys, and the school officers and employees. The most important exception to these usual exclusions occurred in the New York consolidation, in which numerous school systems were combined and made part of the consolidated government.

Consolidated Areas Smaller than Metropolitan Areas

With the exception of the recently completed Baton Rouge consolidation, no consolidated government now encompasses as much as one-fifth of the metropolitan area in which it is located. The metropolitan areas of which the New York and Philadelphia consolidations are parts cross the boundaries of two states.

Not Complete Answers to the Metropolitan Problem

Most consolidations have not proven to be complete solutions to the metropolitan problem. In all the areas involved except Baton Rouge, other methods of coping with metropolitan difficulties subsequently have been adopted or strongly advocated. The shifting of interest in these areas has resulted largely from the inability of consolidated governments to expand their territory at all or significantly since they began functioning. Such territorial stagnation is principally the outgrowth of the absence of state constitutional or legislative permission to enlarge the consolidations. Moreover, consolidated governments located in a section of one state that is part of an interstate metropolitan area have so far found state lines to be insurmountable barriers to growth. No interstate arrangements exist that provide a legal basis for establishment of a consolidated government of metropolitan scope across state lines.

Despite the lack of ability of consolidated governments to keep pace with metropolitan expansion, there has not been serious consideration of discarding consolidation where it is in operation. Instead, other devices are used or suggested as supplements or reinforcements to the consolidation arrangements.

Rejected Consolidation Proposals

The small number of consolidations in metropolitan areas, however, does not reflect the amount of interest that has been expressed in this approach to the metropolitan problem. This is clearly indicated by an analysis of the period since 1920. During these years only one consolidation has been adopted, but many others have reached various stages of consideration. Many times interest has not proceeded beyond discussion, study or recommendation by groups and individuals such as grand juries, leagues of women voters, civic associations, chambers of commerce, junior chambers of commerce, newspapers, city-county official committees, city officials, and county officials. Activity of this nature has occurred in the Atlanta, Austin, Charlotte, Durham, Houston, San Antonio and Toledo metropolitan areas, among others.[12]

[12] Some of these areas subsequently have turned to other metropolitan devices or currently have new studies under way of consolidation alone or in connection with other possibilities.

In many instances actual attempts to install city-county consolidation have had to involve (1) passage of a state constitutional amendment or a state enabling act, or both, and (2) consent of the local voters. These conditions were not present in combination in any of the consolidations that became operative in the last century; all of them were put into effect exclusively through state legislation. Since 1920, in all serious consolidation activities except that of Baton Rouge, one or more of these conditions were unattainable. Unlike all consolidations that are in operation, moreover, two (and occasionally more) local popular majorities are required under many existing state constitutional provisions and laws.

Inability to Gain Authorization

Numerous consolidation efforts in recent years have been stopped at an early point, before submission to the voters, by failure to gain legislative approval of the proposed constitutional or legislative authorization. Among consolidation movements halted in this way were proposals relating to King County (Seattle) in 1923, Ramsey County (St. Paul) in 1924, Cuyahoga County (Cleveland) in 1925, the Boston area in 1931, Jackson County (Kansas City, Missouri) in 1933, Wyandotte County (Kansas City, Kansas) in 1937, and Milwaukee County (Milwaukee) in 1937.[13]

Voter rejection of proposed constitutional amendments has blocked the adoption of some consolidation proposals that had obtained legislative consent. Demise occurred at this stage through decisions of the state-wide electorate in consolidation plans, for example, concerned with Multnomah County (Portland, Oregon) in 1927, Jefferson County (Birmingham) in 1936 and 1948, and Jefferson County (Louisville) in 1937. The latter two were defeated by decisive margins of three to one and ten to one, respectively. A proposed constitutional amendment to permit consolidation of Dade County, Miami, two villages, and a town was turned down by the voters of Dade County in 1948 in balloting that determined whether they favored its submission in a state election. Had these amendments been approved by the voters of the various states, the consolidation proposals in general would have taken the form of local charters or state legislative plans of government subject to local voter approval.

[13] Consolidation proposals are usually identified in this discussion by the county or counties and the most populous city involved. In some proposals additional local governments have been part of the consolidation.

The Metropolitan Record: Consolidation

Legislative and Local Inaction

Some attempts at consolidation surmount these legislative and statewide election requirements but succumb before a local election is held. Defeat at this point develops in one of two ways. One is failure of the state legislature to pass implementing legislation after the amendment is approved by the state voters, a situation that occurred, for example, in Washington subsequent to passage of a constitutional amendment in 1948. The second is failure to use the authorization locally. A constitutional amendment passed in Texas in 1933 is an illustration of lack of local activity at this step in the process. Not one of the numerous counties eligible to adopt city-county consolidation has done so since adoption of the amendment. Local disinterest in using authorization to consolidate, however, is not always the result of local inertia. It may be attributable to conditions imposed in the authorization, such as a difficult vote to effect consolidation or a limitation on the taxing power of the consolidated government.

Rejection by Local Voters

Since 1920, apparently only five attempts at city-county consolidation other than the successful Baton Rouge plan have survived until the final step of local approval. Prior to the local election, each of them had gained the necessary authorization from either the legislature or the state electorate or both. Although all that remained was to acquire the consent of the local voters, none received the requisite majority or majorities in the local election. A St. Louis-St. Louis County proposition of 1926 received one of two required majorities. In 1950 a Newport News-Warwick County-Elizabeth City County plan obtained two of the five majorities it needed. A measure to consolidate Dade County and Miami by abolishing the City of Miami lost by less than 1,000 votes in 1953. The other two city-county consolidation attempts in metropolitan areas that were rejected in local elections occurred in Bibb County (Macon, Georgia) in 1933 and Duval County (Jacksonville) in 1935.

The Defeats in Retrospect

Certain features stand out prominently in the city-county consolidation attempts defeated at the legislative, constitutional amendment and local election stages. In many instances the legal authorization did not exist at the time local interest became serious; consequently an effort, frequently unsuccessful, had to be made to gain permission. Most of the legal authorizations were and are applicable to one designated county or to certain counties possessing a specified minimum population. Typically, the rejected consolidations—with only a few exceptions, such as the Newport News-Warwick County-Elizabeth City County plan—related to a single county; they were not intercounty even when the metropolitan area currently covered two or more counties. The one-county territorial limitation is usually the result of state constitutional and legislative provisions that do not allow city-county consolidation on an intercounty basis.

Many of the consolidation proposals involved the merger of the government of the county's most populous city with that of the county; smaller municipalities were not included. Many consolidation plans could be adopted only after two separate popular majorities were obtained, one in the city or incorporated areas involved, the other in the remainder of the county. Under this requirement of dual approval, an over-all majority, such as was obtained for the St. Louis measure in 1926 by a two-to-one margin, was insufficient.

City-County Consolidation: An Appraisal

The greatest merit of the city-county consolidation approach lies in providing a unified, coordinated program of service, development and control over an area larger than that previously served exclusively by one general local government. It eliminates duplication of certain services formerly provided by both city and county governments, and consequently it is financially attractive, particularly when municipalities occupy most of the territory that is consolidated.

Because city-county consolidation provides this larger governmental jurisdiction, various metropolitan areas have had initial and sometimes recurring interest in the device. But, in spite of a number of recent and current consolidation studies and plans, attempts to consolidate have been less frequent since 1940 than in the two previous decades.

The almost universal difficulty of gaining adoption of such proposals has been one major contributor to the relative shift from this approach to other possibilities. Frequently a state constitutional amendment involving state-wide popular approval must be sought or legislative authorization must be obtained. If such legal permission is acquired, in many instances it contains a local voting procedure calling for dual ma-

The Metropolitan Record: Consolidation

jorities. Gaining legal authority or local consent or both has proved extremely difficult. Meantime, the metropolitan problem has remained or grown larger, and in many areas efforts have been turned to other approaches.

There have been other contributing factors as well. Especially as the cities in metropolitan areas have grown in number, opposition to city-county consolidation has increased and interest has lagged. This is because it represents the complete elimination of many incorporated areas and the vesting of all local autonomy in a single government that can be remote from important needs and points of view in localities within its jurisdiction. As a result, consolidation is regarded by some individuals and groups as simply annexation under a different name. Opposition also crystallizes when the territory to be consolidated contains a substantial amount of rural land and when there is a state legal requirement, as is the situation in many states, that taxation must be uniform throughout the consolidated area.

One additional factor—the area limitation in most consolidation proposals that have been adopted or defeated—deserves emphasis because it restricts the general usefulness of city-county consolidation. Practically all consolidations have been formulated on a single county basis, in accordance with territorial provisions in the constitutional or legislative authorizations. Such an area restriction makes the consolidation device inadequate for the sizable number of metropolitan areas that are intercounty and lie within one state. It has been very difficult, in most instances impossible, to enlarge the original boundaries of consolidations subsequently. Moreover, no interstate arrangements exist to furnish the legal basis for consolidation plans for interstate metropolitan areas.

Under present legal conditions, city-county consolidation seldom will be an attractive and practical approach except in certain medium and small metropolitan areas that contain the territory of one county and seem unlikely to become intercounty. To make city-county consolidation usable comprehensively in many metropolitan areas will require major changes in state constitutional and statutory provisions and the adoption of new interstate arrangements.

3. City-County Separation

City-county separation is distinguishable from city-county consolidation and deserves independent consideration. Such separation involves the detachment of a city, in some instances after territorial enlargement, from the rest of a county.[1] The separated government performs both municipal and county functions, although in some cases not all of the latter. Many activities formerly carried on by two governments are unified, but only in the area that is detached from the remainder of the county.

Although advocated in far fewer metropolitan areas, city-county separations are more numerous than city-county consolidations. Separated governments are in operation in Baltimore, Denver, St. Louis and San Francisco as a result of local sponsorship. They are also functioning, through an automatic legal process, in all cities in Virginia, including its seven central cities of metropolitan areas. The first four warrant analysis as a group apart from the Virginia examples.

Comparison of Four City-County Separations

Not of Recent Origin

Not one of these four separations was activated during the last half-century, and most of them are quite old. Two of them started in the middle of the last century, Baltimore's in 1851 and San Francisco's in 1856. Separation followed in St. Louis in 1876. It became operative in Denver in 1902, but because of court litigation not fully effective until about a decade later.

Usually Based on Constitutional Change

Obtaining state constitutional authorization was necessary in efforts for city-county separation in Baltimore, St. Louis and Denver. Separation became legally possible in Baltimore and St. Louis through provisions contained in new state constitutions adopted by the voters. It was

---

[1] Along lines similar to city-county separation as discussed in this section, but broader in scope, are proposals made in Chicago, Detroit and New York a number of years ago. They called for separation of a city and the adjacent area from both the county and the state and the formation of city-states. None of them progressed very far.

made available to Denver through a constitutional amendment. Although founded on state constitutional sections, each separation was placed in effect in a different way. The constitutional amendment relating to Denver was self-executing upon issuance of a proclamation by the governor. In the Baltimore separation, enactment of supporting state legislation was necessary, and in the St. Louis arrangement an over-all popular majority in the city and the county had to be obtained. The latter proposal was the only one of the four that required strictly local voter consent.

In contrast to the others, the San Francisco separation did not involve obtaining a constitutional basis. An act of the legislature was deemed sufficient, since it was not in conflict with any part of the state constitution which had been recently adopted. Twenty-three years later, however, provision for separation and confirmation of San Francisco's existing status were included as original provisions in a new state constitution.

Addition of Territory at Time of Separation

Territorial enlargement of the detached city has ordinarily been part of the separation process. The lone exception among the four examples under consideration is Baltimore, which separated with exactly the same boundaries that had existed previously. St. Louis and San Francisco were expanded about threefold and fourfold, respectively, but the addition to Denver was more modest. The method of acquisition employed in St. Louis was unique. A locally elected board of city charter drafters had the exclusive right to determine the size of the area, which then was included as a part of the separation plan submitted to a combined city and county popular vote. The St. Louis separation was unusual, also, in that it alone provided for differential tax rates in the new areas, a practice that was later eliminated. In total, most of the territory absorbed by the three cities at the time of separation was unincorporated. This was the status of all land allocated to San Francisco and St. Louis; Denver, on the other hand, obtained both unincorporated and incorporated (town) territory.

Disposition of Remainder of County

Generally, a single county was established in all the area of the previous county that remained after separation. Such was the development in the Baltimore, San Francisco and St. Louis separations. The remainder of the county not made part of San Francisco was organized as San Mateo County; in the other two instances, the newly formed counties retained the names they had before separation. The official titles would be of little consequence except that retention of identical names by counties and separated cities can lead to confusion. Thus the City of Baltimore is situated outside of but adjacent to Baltimore County, and the City of St. Louis is not in St. Louis County. Unlike the other three separations, Denver's detachment did not involve continuance of the rest of the county as a single unit; instead, some portions were established as two new counties, and others were attached to several existing counties.

The territory of the county not included in the area that detaches is sometimes identified in discussions of city-county separation as the "rump" county or "residue." These terms are accurate in the sense that the territory is not part of the land that separates. However, the designations may be interpreted mistakenly to mean that the area that separates has acquired most of the territory of the county in which it was previously located. This has never been the situation. The "rump" county, although lightly populated, always has exceeded the territorial size of the separated area by eight or more times when the separation went into effect.

Subsequent Additions of Territory

Usually no territory, or only a moderate amount, has later been annexed to the separated area. The boundaries of San Francisco and St. Louis are the same as they were in 1856 and 1876 when the separations were completed. No provision was made in the separation process for them to acquire territory located in another county.

In St. Louis the tripling of the city's area at the time of separation was regarded as making future boundary extensions unnecessary. Within a few decades, however, rapid population growth was occurring in St. Louis County from which St. Louis had separated, and numerous mutual problems developed. It was not until 1924 that a constitutional amendment was adopted permitting the territorial readjustment of St. Louis and St. Louis County. Three options were provided: city-county consolidation, re-entry of the city into the county, or annexation of part of the county by the city.[2] Two years after passage of the amendment, a city-county consolidation plan calling for the absorption of all county territory by the city was submitted to the local voters. Requiring separate popular majorities in the city and in the county, the plan passed decisively in the city and was even more decisively rejected in the county.

In 1930 another constitutional amendment was proposed. It would have enabled the areas of the City of St. Louis and St. Louis County to merge under a new metropolitan government plan in which the existing incorporated places would continue and perform strictly local functions. Specific details were never determined or voted on locally because the proposed amendment was defeated in a state-wide election. No subsequent proposition to change the territory of St. Louis has been submitted to popular vote.

The voting procedure available for territorial merger of San Francisco with all or part of San Mateo County, from which it separated in 1856, is even more difficult. A provision, written into the constitution many years after the separation, requires that many separate majorities be obtained in order to annex or consolidate incorporated and unincorporated territory in the county with San Francisco. Popular majorities are necessary in each incorporated city in the county area involved, in the entire county, and in San Francisco. Moreover, if only a part of San Mateo County is to be merged with San Francisco, over-all majority consent must be acquired in the territory to be detached. Although a merger plan was seriously discussed around 1930, and some of its provisions were included in the San Francisco charter that was adopted in 1931, no proposal ever has been submitted to the area voters.

Denver, which was not substantially enlarged at the time of separation, subsequently has made a number of small annexations in two different counties, under fairly difficult state legislation. In contrast to the cities in the other three separations, Denver always has had the legal power to annex. The constitutional amendment permitting separation stipulated that the general state laws relating to absorption of incorporated and unincorporated areas were applicable. When absorbed, territory automatically detaches from the county in which it has been located and becomes a part of the separated area.

[2] The new state constitution of 1945 included these three alternatives and added a fourth option in the field of city-county relations. The fourth, which permits establishment of one or more metropolitan special districts to handle area service needs, was utilized in 1954 to create a metropolitan sewer district encompassing St. Louis and the densely settled portion of St. Louis County.

Of the four separated cities, only Baltimore has later gained considerable territory. The separation development in this area has been unusual in several ways. Baltimore obtained no additional territory in detaching from the county and began its separate existence with less than one-third as much land as any of the other three separated cities initially possessed. Annexations of 1888 and 1918, providing temporary tax differentials in the annexed areas, were accomplished through special acts of the legislature. The acts were vigorously opposed in two counties which lost territory as a result of them, and were unsuccessfully challenged in the courts. The right of the state legislature to effect simi-

TABLE 7

AREA AND POPULATION OF FOUR SEPARATED GOVERNMENTS, COUNTIES FROM WHICH SEPARATED, AND METROPOLITAN AREAS

Governmental unit or metropolitan area	Area in square miles	Population
Baltimore................	79	949,708
Baltimore County........	610	270,273
Metropolitan area........	1,106	1,337,373
Denver..................	66	415,786
Arapahoe County.........	820	52,125
Metropolitan area........	2,918	563,832
St. Louis................	61	856,796
St. Louis County.........	497	406,349
Metropolitan area........	2,520	1,681,281
San Francisco............	45	775,357
San Mateo County........	454	235,659
Metropolitan area........	3,314	2,240,767

Source: United States Bureau of the Census, *Local Government in Metropolitan Areas*, State and Local Government Special Studies No. 36 (Washington: 1954), pp. 8, 9, 13. The areas are for 1952 and the populations for 1950. Arapahoe County constitutes only a part of the county in which Denver formerly was situated.

lar annexations remains but has been unused for many years. Apparently the opposition of the adjacent counties, now more heavily populated, would be stronger than before against such a proposal.

Not Metropolitan in Scope

The four separated governments currently contain merely a portion of the metropolitan areas, as defined by the Census Bureau, of which they are the central cities. None possesses even one-seventh as much territory as the county from which it detached. Moreover, each of the metropolitan areas involved includes far more than the territory of both the separated government and the county of which it previously was a part. Consequently, no separated government covers one-twelfth of the metropolitan area, and one embraces as little as approximately 1½ per cent.

A similar situation is noticeable regarding distribution of population in the metropolitan areas, although to a lesser degree. Two of the separated governments contain about seven-tenths of the people living in the metropolitan areas in which they are located; one has slightly less than one-half, and the fourth, approximately one-third. On the basis of relative amounts of territory and population, none of the separated governments can be considered a government of metropolitan jurisdiction.

City-County Separation in Virginia

Three Differences

City-county separation in Virginia differs in three respects from the previously discussed examples. First, there has never been a legal authorization in Virginia directly providing for city-county separation, although constitutional and statutory provisions recognize the principle and the state's highest court in several instances has given tacit approval to the practice. As Chester W. Bain has noted, this long-established procedure "gradually evolved until it reached its present-day form . . . it is simply the product of usage."[3]

Second, separation from the county is an automatic process applicable to any city in the state that attains a population of 5,000. It does not apply to towns which consist of incorporated places of less than 5,000 inhabitants and those of 5,000 or more that have not requested a change to city status. Third, city-county separation is more comprehensive in cities of 10,000 or more than in the less populous cities. Cities of 10,000 or more are completely separate from the county and are in no way subject to county jurisdiction or taxation. Within their boundaries they perform all functions, including the administration of justice, previously carried out by the county. Cities containing 5,000 to 10,000 people (and a few of less population that possessed city charters before adoption of

[3] Chester W. Bain, "Annexation in Virginia: The Use of the Judicial Process for Readjusting City-County Boundaries" (Charlottesville: University of Virginia Bureau of Public Administration, 1955, typewritten manuscript), pp. 30, 33.

the present constitution in 1902) are territorially separate from the county but share the circuit court of the county of which they were formerly a part. Each of these less populous cities and the county from which it is separated utilize and share in paying for the services of the same judge, court clerk and commonwealth's attorney. In all other activities and financial affairs, they are independent of the county.

Use of Annexation

Virginia cities are not granted additional territory when detaching, but their boundaries can be extended subsequently through annexation. Before 1902 such a change required the passage of a special legislative act. In accordance with provisions in a new constitution adopted in 1902, the legislature two years later passed a general act providing for a special three-judge court to determine the merits of individual annexation proposals. If the court enters a favorable order, the territory (which may include towns as well as unincorporated areas) is annexed to the city and ceases to be within the county.[4]

Thirty-two cities in Virginia, including the seven central cities of metropolitan areas, are separate from the counties. Under the judicial annexation process whose availability parallels the period of major growth of metropolitan areas in the state, five metropolitan central cities have each obtained territory on from three to five occasions. Collectively they have annexed slightly more than half of the total of 201 square miles obtained by all cities in Virginia. However, almost three-fourths of the court judgments ordering annexations to these five cities involved less than five square miles each. The two other central cities came into legal existence in 1952 and have not grown territorially.

Effects of Boundary Changes

The continuing absorption of county territory by separated governments is producing effects not anticipated during the early years of the judicial annexation process. For example, the repeated activities of one central city in proposing or completing annexations in neighboring counties recently brought on extraordinary protective action by two counties that could be a prelude to similar activity by other counties. In 1950 a proposed consolidation of the City of Newport News, the

[4] An analysis of the Virginia annexation process is contained in the section on annexation.

The Metropolitan Record: Separation

City of Hampton, the Town of Phoebus and the Counties of Warwick and Elizabeth City received an over-all majority of votes cast in the area, but failed to obtain popular majorities in each affected governmental unit as required by the state enabling act. Two years later, through local voter consent, one of the counties incorporated as a city and the other incorporated and consolidated with a city and a town. Warwick County became the City of Warwick. Elizabeth City County, the City of Hampton and the Town of Phoebus converted into the new City of Hampton. The two new cities are the largest in area in the state. The major purpose of these actions was to prevent the central city of Newport News from annexing additional county territory. Under Virginia's annexation procedure unincorporated areas and entire towns can be absorbed but cities are immune. As a result of these changes, the three cities of Newport News, Warwick and Hampton together encompass the entire metropolitan area of the Lower Peninsula.

The annexing of county area by separated governments seems about to produce other important repercussions. "The time is not too far distant," Chester Bain has stated, "when annexation courts will be faced with an obvious need by a city for annexation of territory in a county which after annexation would be insufficient in area, population, and taxable resources to continue operation as a primary, political subdivision but too large to be added to the annexing city."[5] He also concludes that, as the metropolitan problem becomes more acute and additional towns convert to city status and automatically separate from counties, "rather radical adjustments will have to be made in Virginia's pattern of local government."[6]

Negligible Recent Interest

Little or no interest in utilizing city-county separation has emerged in most metropolitan areas during the present century. Only one election on the question has occurred since the Denver action of 1902. In 1922, three months after voter disapproval of a county-wide merger

[5] Chester W. Bain, "Annexation: Virginia's Not-So-Judicial System," *Public Administration Review*, 15 (Autumn, 1955), p. 261.

[6] *Ibid.*, p. 262. One provision of a constitutional amendment proposed in 1955 by the Virginia Advisory Legislative Council but rejected in the legislature would have raised from 5,000 to 10,000 the population minimum needed by newly incorporated towns to become cities and consequently to gain separate status, protection from annexation, and authority to annex towns and unincorporated county territory.

plan, a proposal to separate Oakland and two small cities from the remainder of Alameda County (in the eastern section of the San Francisco Bay metropolitan area) was decisively defeated. Elsewhere, activity in support of separation has seldom reached an advanced stage.

The most serious separation efforts materialized in two central cities of metropolitan areas in California. In 1932 the Los Angeles city council passed an ordinance petitioning the county board of supervisors to submit a separation measure to the voters of both the city and county. The assistant county counsel ruled the council action illegal; a survey by a county research agency declared the plan unfeasible and financially hazardous; and widespread opposition arose outside of the city. The proposition was not placed on the ballot. Seven years later, in an advisory vote on the question of separation from the county, voters of the City of San Diego rejected the proposition by more than three to one.

Occasionally a state constitutional amendment is proposed to authorize both city-county consolidation and separation. The Washington electorate in 1948 adopted such an amendment, restricted to King County (Seattle). The legislature, however, has not enacted supplementary legislation providing the method of local voting on either option or the procedure for determining the boundaries if separation is used. An amendment applicable exclusively to Multnomah County (Portland), and including both alternatives, was defeated by Oregon's voters in 1927.

Infrequently, a separation measure is introduced in a state legislature, such as a bill in Minnesota's 1950 session to detach Minneapolis from Hennepin County. More often, but still infrequently, a private group or an official in a city simply urges the city to "secede" from the county. A proposal along these lines was presented to the city commissioners (city council) of Salt Lake City in 1950.

All of these types of activity in support of city-county separation add up to a very small total. It is evident that far fewer proposals advocating utilization of this device have been made in the twentieth century than for any other major approach to the metropolitan problem. City-county separation has been in a long period of eclipse that may be permanent.

City-County Separation: An Appraisal

The major advantage of city-county separation is financial benefit to the city that severs from the county. It abolishes the practice of the county spending in unincorporated areas part of the taxes collected in the city. It also reduces the amount of duplication of functions previously performed by two different governments. Two related factors may be present, however. Some counties, in losing valuable tax resources, experience great difficulty in meeting service demands, certain of which are intensified by geographical proximity to the separated area. Some separated governments cannot be organized with optimum effectiveness because constitutional provisions require certain county activities to be rendered independently within the separated city.

In general, city-county separation has serious shortcomings as a method of meeting the metropolitan problem. By the nature of the approach, a separated area at the time of its formation cannot encompass an entire county, for this represents consolidation and not separation. Usually separated governments have obtained no increase in territory when separating. Separation could, however, still become a useful device in metropolitan situations if sufficient territory could be annexed later. This has not taken place following actual separations. St. Louis and San Francisco have encountered severe and seemingly insurmountable constitutional obstacles to annexation. Baltimore has possessed no consistently and readily available procedure and has had to depend on special actions of the state legislature. Denver and the Virginia cities have been able to utilize annexation processes but have registered territorial gains that are small in relation to the size of their metropolitan areas. Elsewhere in many states where separation is not in operation, its use would not be effective in metropolitan areas unless accompanied by major legal changes to permit cross-county annexations and the absorption of incorporated places.

Separation usually increases the number of governmental units; even more important, it removes the city from a position of influence in the county, which is a larger local government area. Yet, in practically every instance the county from which a city has separated is now a part of the same metropolitan area. As an act of withdrawal, city-county separation is a step backward from attainment of a governmental jurisdiction of metropolitan scope. It cannot be regarded as a generally effective approach to the metropolitan problem.

4. Federation (The Borough Plan)

The basic element of federation, or the borough plan, is the division of functions between a newly created metropolitan government and the existing municipalities within its territory. The new metropolitan government, generally possessing the same territorial limits as the replaced county government, is assigned metropolitan-type functions. The municipal governments—sometimes enlarged in area and called boroughs—continue in existence and exercise legislative and administrative discretion and control over local functions. Moreover, in all proposed federations seriously considered in the United States, local representation on the governing body of the metropolitan government has been specified. This is accomplished by requiring distribution of membership of the governing body on the basis of residence in, or election or appointment from, areas smaller than the entire territory within the federation.[1]

Federation has been advocated as a logical and suitable solution that fulfills the need for a general metropolitan jurisdiction while retaining more localized governments for local governmental activities. However, the broad popular appeal that its advocates have expected for it has not so far materialized. Among all the frequently discussed approaches, federation is the only one that has yet to be instituted in a single metropolitan area in the United States.[2]

Attempts at Federation

Few Serious Efforts

Despite the extensive support federation has received in general discussions and writings, few attempts have been made to adopt it in spe-

[1] The urban county and the metropolitan special district approaches, discussed in later sections, in some instances represent types of federation. Even in these cases, however, they deviate from at least one of the characteristics (such as abolition of an existing county governmental unit) of the type of federation proposals under discussion here, and many times they are far less comprehensive.

[2] New York City is an illustration of consolidation and not federation because the local boroughs do not have legislative powers. Regrettably for purposes of easy understanding, use of the word "borough" is not reserved exclusively for federation plans. It may designate an area utilized for either election or administrative purposes or for the channeling of neighborhood needs and opinions. It also may refer to one of the regular types of local governments operating in certain states, including Pennsylvania and New Jersey. None of these four uses constitutes federation (the borough plan).

The Metropolitan Record: Federation

cific metropolitan areas, and few have progressed very far. Federation was first seriously proposed in 1896. A three-member commission appointed by the governor of Massachusetts to study forms of metropolitan organization recommended passage of a legislative bill calling for a referendum on the federation question in the Boston area. The bill did not pass, and federation received little attention in any metropolitan area for about two decades. In 1916 a movement developed in Alameda County (Oakland) and reached an unsuccessful climax five years later when the local electorate turned down a federation charter.[3]

The second and last federation proposal that has been voted on as a local election proposition was rejected by the electorate of Allegheny County (Pittsburgh) in 1929. In the following year a proposed constitutional amendment authorizing the drafting of a federation charter, to be submitted locally in St. Louis and St. Louis County, was defeated in a state-wide election. A detailed plan was formulated for San Francisco and San Mateo County during the 1920's and was partially incorporated into a new San Francisco charter adopted in 1931; the plan, however, never was submitted to local voter decision. Two federation bills relating to the Boston area were before the Massachusetts legislature in 1931, but it failed to enact either.

Another long period of inactivity followed, interrupted only by abortive attempts at revival during the 1930's in the San Francisco-San Mateo area, Alameda County, and Allegheny County. Finally, in 1955, a plan of federation for Dade County, prepared by a professional consulting organization, received unanimous approval from a city-county board created by the City of Miami. A constitutional amendment authorizing federation and other types of metropolitan reorganization was proposed, but the state legislature altered the amendment to make the board of county commissioners the governing body of the metropolitan government.[4] A locally drawn charter, to be voted on by the county electorate in November, 1956, will become operative only if the proposed constitutional amendment is approved simultaneously at a state-wide election.

Excluding the Boston area proposals which concerned an entire county and parts of three others, all federation plans have related to a single

---

[3] The Alameda County and the San Francisco-San Mateo area federation attempts are analyzed in John C. Bollens, *The Problem of Government in the San Francisco Bay Region* (Berkeley: University of California Bureau of Public Administration, 1948), pp. 65–95. Studies of the Boston, Pittsburgh and St. Louis areas have been made but not published.

[4] Several features of the Dade County development that preceded the legislative change are reviewed in this section on federation. The legislative action transformed the federation plan to the urban county classification which is the approach considered in the next section.

county or to a separated government and the county of which it previously was a part. The Alameda County, Allegheny County and Dade County proposals are illustrations of the one-county concept. The San Francisco-San Mateo County proposition in its most advanced form and the St. Louis-St. Louis County plan are illustrations of the separated government-former county arrangement.

Division of Functions

No common pattern has been followed in allocating functions between the metropolitan government and the municipal governments or in the method of distribution employed. The Alameda County and the San Francisco-San Mateo area plans enumerated the powers to be exercised by the municipal governments or boroughs, thus reserving all other functions to the metropolitan government. Under the proposed Alameda County charter, the boroughs could (1) enact local ordinances to protect the general welfare of persons within their boundaries, (2) appropriate funds for street repair and maintenance, sewer construction exclusive of main sewers, police and fire maintenance, and incidental expenses of borough officials, (3) assume bonded indebtedness upon approval by a two-thirds vote of the borough voters, (4) undertake borough improvements financed through special assessments, and (5) investigate the expenditure of borough funds by borough officials and departments. The boroughs were specifically prohibited from acting on traffic, planning, harbor development, building regulation, and licenses other than liquor licenses.

The powers enumerated for the municipal governments or boroughs in the San Francisco-San Mateo area proposal were to (1) create zoning and planning areas, (2) construct and maintain public libraries, parks, local sewers and public buildings, (3) construct, improve and maintain streets, bridges and sidewalks, (4) enact local police ordinances, and (5) incur indebtedness for public improvements.

In contrast to the allocation procedure employed in the Alameda County and the San Francisco-San Mateo area plans, the federation charter for Allegheny County enumerated the powers of the metropolitan government, reserving all other activities to the municipal governments. In addition to assuming the powers of the replaced county government, the metropolitan government could (1) supply by means of special tax district financing any utility or service not exclusively for the use of one governmental unit in the area, (2) construct and maintain through streets and control the traffic on them, (3) construct and operate transportation systems for passenger, freight or express traffic, (4) own and operate water works, and purchase municipally-owned works upon the consent of the voters of the municipality, (5) operate a police department to function in addition to local police forces, (6) regulate smoke, (7) formulate the main features of a master plan for the feder-

TABLE 8

PROPOSED DIVISION OF FUNCTIONS BETWEEN METROPOLITAN AND MUNICIPAL GOVERNMENTS IN THE DADE COUNTY (FLORIDA) FEDERATION PLAN

Metropolitan Government	Municipal Governments
Policy Formulation	
Policies affecting Metropolitan Miami.	Policies concerning local affairs.
Executive Management	
Management of metropolitan government.	Management of municipal governments.
Planning	
Metropolitan planning; technical assistance to municipalities.	Municipal planning within the framework of metropolitan plans.
Financial Administration	
Financial administration for metropolitan government.	Financial administration for municipal governments.
Property assessment and property tax collection and distribution for all local governments.	
Personnel Administration	
Personnel administration for metropolitan government; technical assistance to municipalities.	Personnel administration for municipal governments.
Legal Services	
Legal services to metropolitan government.	Legal services to municipal governments.
Streets and Highways	
Development and maintenance of arterials and major off-street parking facilities; construction, maintenance, cleaning and lighting of local roads and streets in the unincorporated area.	Construction and maintenance of local municipal streets and of secondary off-street parking facilities. Street cleaning and lighting within corporate limits.

Source: Public Administration Service, *The Government of Metropolitan Miami* (Chicago: 1954), pp. 89–90.

TABLE 8—*Continued*

Metropolitan Government	Municipal Governments

Traffic and Transportation

Master traffic engineering plan for Metropolitan Miami.	Traffic engineering for local municipal streets.
Traffic control devices on all arterials and on local roads and streets in the unincorporated area.	Traffic control devices on local municipal streets.
Development and operation of air, water, rail and bus terminals.	
Regulation and control over, and discretionary authority to operate, public transportation systems.	

Building and Zoning

Uniform building and related technical codes for Metropolitan Miami; enforcement in unincorporated area and review of enforcement in municipalities.	Enforcement of uniform building code and development and enforcement of more rigid requirements within municipal boundaries.
Examining and licensing of building contractors.	Development and enforcement of municipal zoning regulations within the framework of metropolitan land-use plan.
Development and enforcement of zoning regulations for unincorporated area.	

Public Housing and Urban Renovation and Conservation

Administration of metropolitan housing authority; technical guidance to local authorities.	Administration of local housing authorities.
Development and supervision of urban renovation and conservation programs for Metropolitan Miami.	Local renovation and conservation within the framework of metropolitan programs.

Flood Control and Surface Drainage

Cooperation and liaison with federal and regional agencies.	Construction and maintenance of local drainage facilities within municipal boundaries.
Development and maintenance of subsidiary works including major storm sewerage systems.	
Construction and maintenance of local storm drains in special assessment districts of unincorporated area.	

Sanitary Sewerage and Sewage Disposal

Full authority to regulate or operate.

Water Service

Full authority to regulate or operate.

TABLE 8—*Continued*

Metropolitan Government	Municipal Governments

Refuse Collection and Disposal

Refuse collection in the unincorporated area.
Full authority to develop and operate refuse disposal facilities within the metropolitan area.

Refuse collection within municipalities.

Light and Power Utilities

Discretionary authority to operate.
Regulatory authority in the metropolitan area.

Discretionary authority to operate.
Regulatory authority within municipal boundaries.

Health and Welfare Services

Basic authority to provide uniform health and welfare programs for metropolitan area.

Discretionary authority to increase standards within municipalities.

Education, Recreation and Library Services

Development and administration of a public education system for Metropolitan Miami.
Development and operation of a metropolitan system of major parks.
Administration of a comprehensive library program for metropolitan area.

Discretionary authority to provide facilities supplemental to those of the metropolitan system.
Basic authority for municipal park and organized recreation programs.
Discretionary authority to provide local library services.

Law Enforcement

Minimum patrol and traffic control throughout the metropolitan area; provision of full patrol services, at cost, in municipalities which choose to abdicate their basic authority.
Development and administration of central training, communications, records, crime investigations, jail and stockade facilities and services.

Basic authority to provide full patrol and traffic control services within municipalities.
Supplemental police training; maintenance of local police records; discretionary authority to investigate crimes committed within municipalities; operation of detention cells.

Fire Protection

Development of uniform fire code for metropolitan area and execution of minimum fire prevention program.
Development and administration of central fire training and communications facilities and services.
Fire fighting on a cost basis within fire service districts of the unincorporated area.

Discretionary authority to increase standards and to administer supplemental fire prevention programs.
Supplemental training for fire personnel.
Fire fighting within corporate limits.

ated area and (8) make and enforce health regulations in units having no health authority.[5]

The Boston area federation plans also specifically enumerated the functions to be assigned to the metropolitan government. Under the 1896 proposal, for example, the initial responsibilities of the metropolitan government were to provide sewage disposal, water supply and distribution, and metropolitan parks—activities previously handled by three state agencies. Subsequently, as needs became evident and upon gaining permission of the state legislature, the metropolitan government was to assume "other duties that were undeniably of a metropolitan character," such as "the maintenance of the main highways or great business roads which pass through two or more municipalities and . . . possibly questions of metropolitan transportation as well as the care of the rivers and water courses and questions of surface drainage where the interests of two or more towns were affected."[6]

The Dade County federation plan approved by the city-county study board enumerated the functions of both the metropolitan government and the municipal governments. Table 8 on page 89, showing the allocations, clearly indicates that neither level of government was to be vested with exclusive authority in many functional fields. Instead, most of them were regarded as local in some phases and metropolitan in others. This proposal, moreover, is the only one that has provided for the transfer of major responsibilities in public education from one or more school districts to the metropolitan government.

Composition of Metropolitan Governing Board

Although varying in specific details, the federation plans have generally been in agreement on three features of the metropolitan governing board. The first point of general concurrence is that the board should consist of relatively few members. Seven members were stipulated in both the Alameda County and the Allegheny County proposals. In Dade County the plan recommended eleven at the outset and expansion to a possible future maximum of twenty-one. Sixteen members were specified in the San Francisco-San Mateo area proposition. Only the plans for the Boston area proposed a much larger governing board; for example, a governing group of 100 to 120 was to be created under the terms of one of the legislative bills considered in 1931.

[5] Studenski, *The Government of Metropolitan Areas*, pp. 380–382.
[6] *Ibid.*, p. 370.

Selection of governing board members by election is the second point of general agreement. All federation plans except two pertaining to the Boston area required direct election. Election was called for in most of the seven alternatives suggested in the Boston report of 1896, but no one option was recommended as preferable. One of the 1931 legislative bills relating to the Boston area specified that the mayors of cities and the chairmen of the boards of selectmen of towns within the federated area were to comprise the membership of the governing board.

The third point of agreement is that each member should be a resident of or elected from a particular area. The Alameda County charter provided for election of members from districts. The Allegheny County plan required election at large of residents from districts. The Dade County proposal suggested election at large of eight members from eight districts, election of two members from the two most populous municipalities, and election at large of the president without restriction as to his residence. Under the San Francisco-San Mateo area proposition, eleven members were to come from San Francisco and five from San Mateo County. The principle of area representation was also carried out in one of the Boston area legislative bills of 1931; it provided for the local mayors and town board chairmen to constitute the metropolitan governing body. Two of the federation plans stipulated that the districts were to be of approximately equal population.

Necessity of Constitutional Authorization

In general, federation proposals have had to be based on constitutional rather than state legislative permission, and specific attempts at adoption have had to be preceded by the gaining of state-wide approval of a constitutional amendment. The Boston area proposals, which were submitted to the legislature, constitute the only exceptions. Constitutional amendments under which the federation plans for Alameda County, the San Francisco-San Mateo area and Allegheny County could proceed were sanctioned by the state voters. A subsequent amendment liberalizing the voting procedure for adoption of federation in Allegheny County also was popularly approved. The lone rejection by the voters of a state was that of the proposed constitutional change to authorize drafting of a federation charter for consideration by the people of St. Louis and St. Louis County. A constitutional amendment, deemed essential for implementing the Dade County federation plan, was transmitted to the state legislature, which modified its provisions.

The constitutional authorization is ordinarily applicable to a single area in a state. Furthermore, this statement of permission may be so worded as to be usable only so long as the specific location meets certain conditions. Consequently the wording of the constitutional amendment —which usually is at least in part the product of the local advocates of federation—may prove an obstacle to a second attempt. Such a situation developed in Alameda County. The supporters of federation in the county drafted a constitutional amendment that was approved in a state election in 1919. The constitutional authorization stipulated that a federation charter could be prepared in a county that had a population of 200,000 or more in 1918, contained one or more cities, and was organized under the general state laws. The county voters, however, defeated a proposed federation charter in 1921. Thirteen years later, in 1934, petitions were circulated for the election of a new board of charter drafters. While the petitions were being checked, a case was brought before the California Supreme Court. The court concluded that the election should not be called because the county, as a result of its adoption of a home rule charter a few years before, no longer met one of the three prerequisites. To regain eligibility to proceed under the constitutional grant that had been locally formulated would first require the annulling of the existing charter through a two-thirds popular majority in the county.

Charter Form

With the exception of the Boston area proposals, which were incorporated in state legislative bills, all federation plans have involved a local charter. The charter process, however, has varied considerably. A locally elected board drafted the Alameda County federation charter for presentation to the local voters. A similar procedure would have been used in the St. Louis-St. Louis County plan if the enabling constitutional amendment had passed. A comparable process was recommended by the city-county board concerned with Dade County government. A commission appointed by the governor prepared the draft of the federation charter for Allegheny County, which was subject to state legislative changes before its submission as a local election measure. In the San Francisco-San Mateo area, federation was to be presented in general terms as a local election proposition rather than in the form of a detailed charter. San Francisco, however, was authorized to take charter action of its own that would be applicable to the subsequent federation. A constitutional grant, successfully utilized in 1931, enabled San Francisco to submit to its own voters a new charter or a charter amendment containing federation provisions that would become operative when the election proposition on federation was approved in the San Francisco–San Mateo area.

Procedure for Adoption by Area Voters

Adoption of federation plans ordinarily has depended upon obtaining more than an over-all majority of the votes cast in the area directly involved. The exceptions were the two Boston area proposals of 1931, which were transmitted to the state legislature for its determination, and the Dade County plan, which recommended a single majority in the entire county.

Dual or multiple majorities were conditions in all other federation attempts. In the St. Louis–St. Louis County area, the requirement was separate voter consent in the county and in the city. The Alameda County plan, the first federation proposal to be put to a popular vote in the United States, had to carry in each city in the county. It lost in nine of the ten cities and was defeated by almost a 10,000 margin in the total county-wide vote. The Allegheny County charter, the other federation plan that has been submitted as a local election measure, required a county-wide majority and a two-thirds majority in each of a majority of the affected municipalities. The measure carried throughout the county by approximately 48,000 votes and thus easily attained the over-all margin. But it failed to obtain the required number of extraordinary majorities—recording them in forty-nine municipalities rather than sixty-two that were needed. Ironically, the charter as originally submitted to the state legislature called for majority approval in two-thirds of the municipalities, but an error in printing the resolution altered the provision for adoption to two-thirds approval in a majority of the municipalities.[7] Had this change not occurred, the Allegheny County federation plan would have been adopted.

The largest number of different types of majorities confronted the San Francisco–San Mateo County proposal, which never progressed to the stage of voter decision. Majorities were needed in each city in San

[7] Joseph T. Miller, chairman of the sponsoring group, explains the circumstances of the change in *National Municipal Review*, 18 (October, 1929), pp. 603–609.

Mateo County to be included in the federation, in San Mateo County, and in San Francisco. If the plan were to involve less than all of San Mateo County, an over-all majority in the part of the county proposed for inclusion also would have been required.

Federation in Action: The Toronto Area

There is much current interest in the federation plan that became operative in the metropolitan area of Toronto, Canada, during 1953. This accomplishment is highly impressive. It occurred in the second most populous urban area in Canada and the fifteenth most populous metropolitan area in North America. It represents one of the few instances of the century in which a heavily populated section of the continent has attained a general governmental organization of metropolitan jurisdiction.

The Background Events

The major developments that led to adoption of federation in the Toronto area are important, and they parallel some of the events that have taken place in a number of metropolitan sectors of the United States. The principal and crucial difference, however, is that in Toronto they led to area reorganization. In 1912, following substantial recent annexations, the City of Toronto decided to halt its policy of absorbing nearby areas as population growth occurred in them. The city officials decided that bringing municipal services in the annexed areas up to city-wide standards was too costly. The decision to avoid further annexations was strictly followed for forty years, and it largely accounted for the establishment of suburban municipalities.

Subsequent to the establishment of Toronto's policy against annexation, population growth became extensive in both the city and the adjacent territory, especially during the first and second world wars. Three large townships bordering the city experienced rapid development, and numerous separate municipal governments were organized. In the years after World War II population increase was very pronounced in settlements near Toronto but nonexistent in the central city. The population of the metropolitan area was growing rapidly, but that of Toronto itself was dropping slightly. By 1952, forty years after adoption of the non-annexation policy, thirteen municipalities—Toronto, which was politically and administratively independent of the county, and twelve immediately adjacent, less populous localities in York County—were functioning in the metropolitan area. Each was concerned with a strictly local pattern of development, and each was largely disinterested in area-wide needs and progress.

During the late 1940's numerous metropolitan problems assumed critical proportions.[8] More than half of the suburban municipalities developed as modest residential areas and lacked substantial industries. Consequently, their locally derived revenues were insufficient at reasonable tax rates to provide many services that their inhabitants needed. Water supplies became deficient. Several of the suburban communities—separated from Lake Ontario, their natural source of water, by Toronto—unsuccessfully tried to use wells to obtain water for their expanding populations. Sewage disposal difficulties similarly became acute. Toronto's sewage facilities were no longer adequate to accommodate the adjoining municipalities, and their residents had to turn increasingly to septic tanks, inadequate for protection of health. There was no system of arterial highways to facilitate the development and serve the needs of the metropolitan area, because the municipal officials disagreed on location and financing. Streets that had long been outmoded proved more and more inadequate to accommodate the increased volume of traffic.

The needs for improved education reached a serious stage. Some localities experienced great difficulty in paying for a minimum level of education. A similarly serious situation prevailed in housing. Toronto had no space for housing development; many suburban communities that had space were unsuitable because they lacked the ability to finance necessary public services. Many metropolitan planning studies, made by the Toronto and York Planning Commission, were ineffective because each municipality was responsible for the determination of planning and zoning policies within its borders.

There was growing recognition of the seriousness of service and financial shortcomings and of the need to solve them, but there was much disagreement over what should be done. Official and unofficial organizations made several reports. The Toronto and York Planning Commission in 1949 issued a publication urging the merger of eight of

[8] Frederick G. Gardiner, "Metropolitan Toronto: A New Answer to Metropolitan Area Problems," in American Society of Planning Officials, *Planning: 1953* (Chicago: 1953), pp. 41–42.

the more populous municipalities. Almost simultaneously the privately-supported Civic Advisory Council published a study of local governmental organization and services, the study having been undertaken at the request of the mayor of Toronto and representatives of most adjoining municipalities. Although the report, the first of three prepared on the subject by the civic council, did not make specific recommendations, it increased public interest in the metropolitan problem.

The official and unofficial reports were important, but the key factor leading to adoption of metropolitan area reform was the existence of the Ontario Municipal Board, a province-appointed (state-appointed) administrative tribunal that reviews various municipal matters, including applications for changes in municipal boundaries. Its closest approximation in the United States is the special annexation court in Virginia. In 1946, Mimico, a suburban municipality, applied to the board for an order creating an area, inclusive of the thirteen municipalities in the metropolitan area, for joint administration of certain services. The application, however, was not immediately ready for hearing. In 1950 Long Branch, another suburban municipality, made application for the merger of five of the suburban localities. In the next month Toronto applied to the board for the progressive unification of the thirteen municipal units.

Judging that the Toronto and Mimico applications were related matters, the board gave priority to the Toronto application, with the understanding that evidence and material submitted at the hearing would be applicable to the Mimico proposal. The Long Branch request was postponed indefinitely. The hearing, begun in June, 1950, was exceptionally long and detailed. It spanned almost a year, during which eighty-five witnesses gave approximately three million words of testimony and submitted nearly three hundred items of evidence. All of the suburban municipalities except Mimico opposed the application. The board took the matter under advisement in June, 1951, but did not announce its findings until January, 1953.

Formulation and Adoption of the Plan

The board denied both the Toronto and Mimico applications, thus completing its responsibilities as laid out in provincial (state) legislation. However, the board felt that "it must assume the responsibility of presenting its own proposals for the organization of a suitable form of metropolitan government in the Toronto area [largely because the present applicants] have clearly established the urgent need for some major reform of the existing system. . . ."[9] The board therefore submitted to the provincial premier and legislature a plan calling for federation of the thirteen municipalities in the metropolitan area. The premier responded favorably and had a bill introduced in the provincial legislature. The measure, which in large part implemented the recommendations of the Ontario Municipal Board, was passed in April, 1953, and the metropolitan council was organized in the same month. The federation went into full effect in this metropolitan area of one and a quarter million people on January 1, 1954.

The Distribution of Functions

Two basic elements of the Toronto federation plan stand out most prominently. The first is the establishment of an area-wide unit of government, the Municipality of Metropolitan Toronto, to perform functions that are metropolitan in nature and essential to the whole area. The second is the continued existence of the City of Toronto and of the twelve suburban municipalities (the latter now separated from York County), all of which undertake functions not assigned to the metropolitan unit, and have representation on the metropolitan governing body. Thus, the metropolitan government overlies the territory of the thirteen municipalities but is by no means a complete substitute for them.

The authority of the metropolitan government, whose powers are specifically enumerated in the legislative act, relate to water supply, sewage disposal, arterial highways, certain health and welfare services, housing and redevelopment, metropolitan parks, and over-all planning. It is also empowered to appoint the governing body of the Toronto Transit Commission, provide and manage a court house and jail, aid in financing education, determine funds to be allotted for school sites and construction, review bond proposals of member municipalities and issue such bonds, and set a uniform assessment rate to serve as the basis of taxation for both metropolitan and local purposes. Important functions reserved to the local municipalities in the federation are law enforcement, fire protection, most public health services, direct public relief,

[9] Ontario Municipal Board, *Decisions and Recommendations* (Toronto: January 20, 1953), p. 42.

libraries and building regulations. In many functional fields the metropolitan government undertakes certain activities, and the municipal governments perform others.

The metropolitan government was granted ownership of all pumping stations, treatment plants, reservoirs and trunk lines used in supplying water. It sells water at wholesale to the municipalities, which own the local distribution mains and supply water to consumers at locally determined retail prices. Similarly, the metropolitan government owns all sewage disposal and treatment plants and disposes of sewage from the member municipalities at a wholesale rate. The municipalities continue to be responsible for the local collection systems and charge local residents for sewage services through general taxes or special charges.

The metropolitan unit has taken over certain highways, such as metropolitan roads, and has begun work on a system of arterial highways, expressways and parkways. The governing body of the metropolitan government appoints the directors of the Toronto Transit Commission, which consolidated all independent systems in the metropolitan area and became the sole supplier of public transportation. In health and welfare, the metropolitan responsibilities are hospitalization of indigent patients, post-sanatorium care for consumptives, provision of homes for the aged and maintenance of wards of children's aid societies. The newly established government must provide and maintain a courthouse and jail.

Through a planning board, the metropolitan government may adopt an area-wide plan which, upon approval of the provincial minister of planning and development, becomes controlling within the member municipalities. The metropolitan government is authorized to undertake public housing and redevelopment projects, but it cannot interfere with the exercise of similar powers by the member municipalities. It may establish metropolitan parks. It provides financial grants to schools which are governed by independent local boards and whose educational activities are coordinated by the independent Metropolitan School Board. It reviews local proposals for purchase of school sites and erection of school buildings and issues bonds against its credit. It scrutinizes the bond proposals of municipalities and floats bonds in its own name. Assessment of property, now applied at a uniform rate throughout the area in both metropolitan and local tax levies, was reassigned from the local municipalities to the new metropolitan level.

The Metropolitan Governing Body

The metropolitan council, the governing body of the new unit, consists of twenty-four or twenty-five members, depending upon whether it decides to select a chairman from among its own number or from outside. When appointed from outside, he votes only in case of a tie; when selected from the membership, he votes on all matters and casts a second and deciding vote in stalemates. He is the chief executive officer of the metropolitan government and is chosen annually. An executive committee serves as the general steering committee of the council.

The City of Toronto has twelve members on the metropolitan council, and the twelve suburban municipalities have an equal total. Toronto's representatives are the mayor, the two out of the four controllers who have received the highest number of votes in the last city-wide election, and the nine aldermen (councilmen) who obtained the largest number of ballots in their respective districts in the last municipal election.[10] The chairmen (mayors or reeves) of the councils of the other municipalities are the suburban representatives.

The metropolitan council must adopt an annual budget for the estimated costs of metropolitan functions, including debt payments on capital improvement bonds. The needed revenues are collected in large part through tax bills issued to the thirteen municipalities. The amounts are determined by applying a uniform tax rate to the aggregate assessment of each municipality, which in turn places the payment in its local budget. In addition, each local municipality determines the local tax levy necessary to finance the services it provides. Taxes of both the metropolitan and the municipal governments are based exclusively on real property. The metropolitan and municipal units also receive per capita grants from the Ontario provincial government.

Praise and Criticism

Federation in the Toronto area has been in operation for only a short time. It has been called both "a noble experiment" and "a political expedient," but it is too early to make conclusive judgments about the arrangement. On the one hand, the chairman of the metropolitan council recently reported that "it remained for the year 1955 to demonstrate

---

[10] The controllers and the mayor make up a board having important financial responsibilities in Toronto city affairs.

that this new type of [metropolitan] government can effectively solve the problems of rapidly expanding metropolitan areas." This judgment seemed to be supported by the accomplishments enumerated by him. Much progress has been recorded in water supply, sewage disposal and arterial highways—three of the primary problems that had prompted establishment of the federation. Pooling the financial resources of the metropolitan area has resulted in substantially lower interest rates on bond issues and millions of dollars in savings.[11]

The Toronto federation plan, on the other hand, has been criticized on several major grounds. It does not assign to the new level of government a number of functions, most notably many health activities and law enforcement, that are generally regarded as metropolitan. No method exists, other than provincial legislative action, to bring about the reallocation of any functions. The jurisdiction of the metropolitan government does not include territory that might soon become part of the Toronto metropolitan area. The plan does not provide directly for improvement of local services in some of the smaller member municipalities. Representation of population on the metropolitan governing body is imbalanced; for example, each suburb has one representative despite a tenfold range in numbers of inhabitants. The system of annual election of municipal officials in all except one municipality makes possible an extensive, quick turnover in the membership of the metropolitan council, thus disrupting the development of consistent policy.[12]

The metropolitan council and its chairman have recently made recommendations for provincial legislation on certain matters that have been criticized. They have asked for study of others. In 1955 the metropolitan council approved a recommendation of a special committee that the provincial government pass an act permitting establishment of a metropolitan police force. In 1956 the council chairman told its members that "the time has come when we should discuss how representation on the metropolitan council can be provided upon a more equitable and realistic basis, bearing in mind the geographical area, population and assessment of the constituent municipalities." He noted his intention to recommend

[11] Frederick G. Gardiner, "An Address to the Inaugural Meeting of the Council of the Municipality of Metropolitan Toronto" (Toronto: January 10, 1956), pp. 1–6, 17.

[12] These criticisms, among several others, are contained in Eric Hardy, "Metropolitan Area Merges," *National Municipal Review*, 42 (July, 1953), pp. 326–329, and Winston W. Crouch, "Metropolitan Government in Toronto," *Public Administration Review*, 14 (Spring, 1954), pp. 85–95.

creation of a committee to consider the formulation of a proper basis of representation, and whether members of the metropolitan council and the chairman should be elected directly, and if so, how.[13] Changes in council structure as well as in its functions, and alterations in the territorial boundaries of the metropolitan unit can be made only through passage of legislation by the provincial government.

Federation: An Appraisal

Federation is designed to establish a general metropolitan jurisdiction without completely merging the local governments involved. In offering this combination, it is unlike any previously discussed method of metropolitan area reorganization. Seemingly, federation should be appealing to many people who are conscious of their metropolitan needs but are convinced that certain activities should be performed in comparatively small local areas. Nevertheless, it is as yet unused in the United States.

The basic difficulty in attempts to adopt federation arises from the nature of the method. Many details that do not concern the proponents of more sweeping proposals, such as city-county consolidation, must be faced in the formulation of federation plans. Important decisions must be made on a number of basic matters. Two of these are particularly prominent as possible centers of controversy that may develop into rallying points of opposition. The first is the distribution of powers between the metropolitan and the strictly local units. This involves determinations as to which level should have enumerated functions, and what aspects of particular functions are metropolitan and what ones are local. The second is the composition of the governing body of the metropolitan unit. It involves judgments on whether population should be the only basis of representation, whether the number of representatives should be proportionate to the population within each local unit, and how to insure adequate representation without making the metropolitan governing body unwieldy in size.

As a result of the spelling out of details, some federation plans have constituted extremely complicated arrangements, and this has led to considerable public misunderstanding. The formulators of federation proposals thus may find themselves in the dilemma of trying to decide

---

[13] Gardiner, "An Address to the Inaugural Meeting of the Council of the Municipality of Metropolitan Toronto," pp. 12, 18.

what is adequate detail but not too much detail. Even certain terms, such as boroughs, which are employed in some plans, may be misunderstood and may lack wide popular appeal.

Attempts to employ federation usually cannot be made until specific state constitutional authorization is obtained. The wording of the constitutional section fixes the maximum geographical limits of any proposed federated area, usually confining the boundaries to a single county or to the total area of a separated government and the county of which it was formerly a part. Under this type of restriction, federation, like most existing and proposed city-county consolidations, is insufficient in metropolitan areas that are intercounty or interstate. Also, as in many uses of city-county consolidation, federation may encounter legal problems or obstacles centering on certain constitutional protections to county offices and activities.

The voting procedure specified in state constitutional authorizations for local adoption of federation is in some instances extremely difficult. Although federation involves less substantial change than city-county consolidation, some federation proposals must surmount a much more severe approval procedure than some city-county consolidation propositions. The Baton Rouge consolidation plan was adopted under a constitutional provision calling for a single over-all vote, and the rejected St. Louis-St. Louis County consolidation measure required separate majorities in the City of St. Louis and in the affected territory outside this city. In contrast to these legal stipulations of one or two majorities are the multiple approvals legally required, and unsuccessfully sought, for federation proposals in Alameda and Allegheny counties and in the San Francisco-San Mateo County area.

Broad flexibility is a great potential merit of federation that is absent in certain other metropolitan reorganization approaches. Usually it is within the power of the local framers of a federation charter to include in the document a method of local initiation and approval of amendments. As conditions and attitudes change, the amending procedure can be used to reallocate functions between the metropolitan and local levels or to reconstitute the membership of the metropolitan governing body. It may be possible in some instances to specify in the locally formulated charter a simpler voting procedure for amending than that required in the constitutional authorization to adopt the plan initially. Territorial expansion of the federated area, however, usually must be preceded by altering the state constitution and, less often, by passage of a state law.

5. FUNCTIONAL TRANSFERS AND JOINT EFFORTS

Transfers of functions and joint efforts among local governments usually have represented the mildest type of approach to the metropolitan problem up to the present time. The transfers involve reallocation of at least one service from one or more local governments to another—most commonly the transfer of a single function from a city to a county government.[1] The joint efforts consist of the combined or cooperative handling of at least one public activity by two or more local governments; most of these actions pertain to a single function in which customarily a county and a city, or two cities, participate. In most instances one of the participating units has final responsibility for the joint operation, and in some cases numerous local governments rather than two take part.

Major Characteristics

Many Variations

Every recent year has witnessed increasing authorizations and use of functional transfers and joint efforts. They vary greatly in basic features. Some are seemingly permanent; others, especially certain joint efforts, are temporary. Some are based on special acts of the state legislature; others on general legislation. Some transfers and joint efforts are completed under authority of the governing bodies or administrators; others require the consent of the local voters. Some joint efforts are highly informal arrangements between department heads; others are formal written agreements. Functional transfers usually are based on mutual consent of the governments involved; some state laws, however, require a specific type of government to assume a function on request for a transfer by a second type of government.

Numerous Functions Involved

Many functions currently are involved in transfers or joint efforts or both. Among the more significant are airports, building inspection, civil

[1] There can also be transfers to special districts and to state governments, but they are less widespread. Metropolitan special districts are considered in the following section.

defense, civil service, corrections, election services, fire protection, flood control, public health work and hospitals. Other important functions include law enforcement (especially communications and identification), libraries, parks and recreation, planning, purchasing, refuse disposal, tax assessment, tax collection, public welfare and water supply.[2] Highly numerous are arrangements pertaining to public health, public welfare, tax assessment and tax collection. A number of functions, such as civil service, tax collection and tax assessment, are not direct services to the public but make such services possible or improve them.

The continuing growth of functional transfers and joint efforts can lead to an exaggerated judgment of their present total effect on the general metropolitan problem. For the most part, they represent action on a single function by only two governments. Their employment so far generally has constituted a decidedly piecemeal approach to the large-scale metropolitan problem, which contains many facets and pertains to many governments.

The Urban or Metropolitan County Movement

Greatly increased advocacy of one variation of this approach to the metropolitan problem has occurred in recent years. It is known as the "urban county" method, which in its most complete form means the transformation of county governments in metropolitan areas into metropolitan units. The term is employed rather loosely and broadly to refer to any one of several developments concerning certain counties. One is the piecemeal transfer of individual functions from other local governments to counties. Another is the gradual expansion of some counties from the status of rural local governments and administrative agents of the state governments to include an array of urban activities that they perform in unincorporated urban areas. A third is the simultaneous granting, preferably after county governmental reorganization, of a number of functions to counties located in metropolitan areas. Urban counties, which might more accurately be termed metropolitan counties, can result at different rates of speed from each of these three de-

---

[2] The extensiveness of the arrangements varies considerably in certain functions. Some civil service agreements, for example, relate to examination work only. Others concern many other phases of personnel work, including classification and compensation plans, rules and regulations, hearings, examinations and general administration.

velopments.[3] Of the three, the third, due to its comprehensiveness, has the greatest possibilities for affecting the metropolitan problem.

Erie and Milwaukee County Actions

Numerous actions and proposals, most of them recent, are evidence of widespread support for the urban county idea. Significantly, many of them are concerned with at least a fairly comprehensive use of the device. Several illustrations will demonstrate the types of developments or proposals that are materializing. In 1947 the local voters approved several propositions that advanced Erie County (Buffalo) toward becoming an extensive urban county. The county health department assumed the health work formerly administered by the City of Buffalo; a county library system was established in anticipation of membership of the libraries of Buffalo and other localities; and the county probation department assumed the activities previously handled by the comparable department in Buffalo.

Many recommendations for transfers from the City of Milwaukee to Milwaukee County have been advocated over a period of two decades. Although several suggestions—those relating to health, library and museum, for example—have not been adopted, several important reallocations of functions to the county—smoke abatement, expressways, stadium, memorial drive and war memorial—have been accepted and are in operation.

The Cuyahoga County Proposal

In 1950 a county charter representing a comprehensive plan for conversion of Cuyahoga County (Cleveland) into an urban county was presented to the local electorate. It called for a number of important changes. Included were transfer to the county of all sewer and water facilities not of a purely local nature, and assumption by the county of the operation of all public airports. The charter also would have granted the county exclusive authority to administer a county-wide program of public assistance and permission to serve as a single administrative area in the field of public health. All of these alterations were to take effect

[3] Specific evidence of the urban county movement is contained in Betty Tableman, *Governmental Organization in Metropolitan Areas* (Ann Arbor: University of Michigan Press, 1951), pp. 140–154, and Victor Jones, "Urban Counties," *Municipal Year Book 1954* (Chicago: International City Managers' Association, 1954), pp. 133–147.

upon adoption of the charter. The county was to be given other important powers that could be exercised only with the approval of the municipalities within its boundaries. These consisted of construction and maintenance of through highways, enforcement of a building code and operation of public transportation systems.

The charter was concerned with structural as well as functional reform. It provided for supplanting the existing county governing body with a new board composed of nine members and responsible for legislative activities. It also provided for abolition of many elective county offices and establishment of an elected county administrator charged with major management responsibilities, including the appointment of most department heads.

To be adopted, the charter needed to obtain four separate majorities—a majority of the votes in the entire county, in Cleveland, in the county outside of Cleveland, and in cities, villages and townships. It obtained none of these majorities but it did receive almost half of the votes tabulated in the first three electoral groupings. The percentages of affirmative ballots cast inside and outside Cleveland were virtually identical.

The Allegheny County Plan

Two of the most thoroughgoing urban county actions are pending in Allegheny County (Pittsburgh) and Dade County (Miami). The Metropolitan Study Commission of Allegheny County, created by the Pennsylvania legislature in 1951, issued its report in 1955. It made three principal types of recommendations.[4] One was for passage of a constitutional amendment by the 1955 and 1957 state legislatures and by the voters in 1957 permitting Allegheny County to draft a home rule charter. A second called for subsequent adoption of an urban county charter. Although preserving the autonomy of all 129 municipalities in the county, the charter, if drafted in accordance with the commission's recommendations, would confer upon the county government the exclusive right of property tax collection. It would further grant the county government authority to establish minimum standards in such fields as subdivision controls, building regulations and sanitary sewage construction. The county would enforce its standards in municipalities that did not require adequate compliance with regulations at least equal to those

[4] Metropolitan Study Commission of Allegheny County, *An Urban Home Rule Charter for Allegheny County* (Pittsburgh: 1955), pp. 9–23.

established by the county government. The charter also would provide for merger at the county level of all air pollution and smoke abatement programs and for county enforcement, when existing agencies were inadequate, of an integrated plan of water supply and distribution.

The third major type of recommendation of the metropolitan study commission consisted of proposals for administrative and legislative action that can be placed in operation before approval of the constitutional amendment and the urban county charter. Of approximately fifty recommendations made in this category, one of the most important is unification of thirty-nine individual mass transit systems into a county transit authority; others include establishment of a county health department, centralized purchasing and a county library system, in all of which municipalities can participate voluntarily. Additional recommendations, consequential but different, are to prohibit new incorporations and encourage the annexing of urbanized areas to adjacent incorporated places.

The commission, after issuing its findings and recommendations, decided to wait until the 1957 legislative session to submit the constitutional amendment. As a result, 1959 is the earliest time at which the constitutional amendment and the urban county charter can be put into effect.

The Dade County Charter

In Dade County (Miami) a charter board is at work preparing an urban county charter that will appear as a local election measure on the November, 1956, ballot. In mid-1955 the Florida legislature passed a proposed constitutional amendment granting Dade County home rule powers, subject to approval of the state voters at the same 1956 election. It also enacted a supplementary law creating the charter commission. The amendment must receive state-wide voter approval, and the charter must obtain a majority vote in the county to become operative. If the amendment passes and the charter fails, one or more charters can be prepared subsequently. If the amendment is rejected, a further charter attempt will have to await legislative passage of a new proposed constitutional amendment.

The proposed constitutional amendment permits considerable latitude in the contents of the charter. The amendment's major restriction is that the board of county commissioners must continue to be the governing body of the county government. Two of its sections are particularly broad. Under one of them the charter can establish a method for transferring to the county government any functions possessed by municipalities or other local governments in the county. Under the other, the charter can alter immediately the boundaries of, or consolidate or abolish, any local governments situated wholly within the county, and it can provide a procedure for comparable changes in the future. The charter must contain a method for the submission of later amendments or revisions to the voters of the county, who are given the exclusive right to modify the adopted charter.

Suburban County Efforts

In some instances the urban county idea is being applied in counties that are located in metropolitan areas but do not include the central city. Actions and plans in St. Louis County and Baltimore County, which lie adjacent to the cities of St. Louis and Baltimore, respectively, are illustrative. In 1950 St. Louis County became the first in the state to adopt a charter under the county home rule section of the constitution of 1945. Its formulation and voter acceptance were in large part a response to the county's growing urbanization. Although it accomplished only moderate reorganization of the county government, the charter created the elective position of county supervisor and made him responsible for several major county services, such as hospitals, public health and public welfare. The charter section most significant for the development of an urban county authorizes the county government to assume the performance of any function provided by another local government except a school district, upon approval of the voters of the affected unit. In 1954 a charter amendment providing for a county police department was approved, and in 1956 the county was furnishing various health services to more than half of the approximately ninety municipalities within its limits.

Similarly, an elected board has drafted a home rule charter for Baltimore County, to be submitted at the November, 1956, election. It provides for election of a county governing body, restricted in its functions to legislative matters, and for election of a county executive who, with the approval of the governing body, will appoint a professionally trained and experienced county administrative officer to handle many affairs of the county. The charter also calls for consolidation and simplification of the county departmental organization. If adopted by the voters, the charter can be highly important to the further development of the urban county idea. This is especially true because Baltimore County contains no incorporated communities and has more than 350,000 residents, many of whom desire urban services and controls; the entire county is without any other general local government.

The Urban County Development in California

Although comprehensive proposals for the simultaneous transfer of several or many functions to county governments are increasing, the most extensive urban county development has taken place in California counties on a piecemeal, function-by-function basis. The state-wide trend is particularly noticeable in counties located in metropolitan areas, and it is most apparent in fast-growing Los Angeles County.

Extensive Use

Approximately 1,700 transfers of functions from cities to counties are in effect in California, involving practically all of the counties and a large share of the incorporated places in the state. They are particularly widespread in public health services, tax assessment, tax collection, prisoner care and law enforcement communications. More than three-fifths of the functional transfers are in effect in the fourteen counties located in metropolitan areas.[5] Los Angeles County accounts for almost two-fifths of all transfers of functions to counties situated in metropolitan areas.[6] Table 9 shows the comparative use of the device in the fourteen counties and the markedly prominent degree of activity by Los Angeles County.

Numerous Legal Authorizations

One major factor facilitating the evolution of many counties in California into urban units has been the number and nature of the legal au-

---

[5] San Francisco is both a city and a county and is therefore not included in the number of counties in metropolitan areas.

[6] A detailed city-by-city list of the functions transferred appears in Los Angeles County Chief Administrative Office, Management Division, *Services Provided by the County of Los Angeles to Cities in Los Angeles County* (Los Angeles: 1955). Lakewood, a recently incorporated city of about 50,000 people and the fifteenth most populous in the state, contracts with the County of Los Angeles for most of its municipal services.

thorizations. The legislature in 1921 passed a general state law enabling such actions, and it has been widely used. Its adoption was preceded and followed by the passage of many state laws which individually related to a single type of functional transfer. In addition, the constitutional amendment of 1911 that made county home rule available to all counties was subsequently amended to permit charter counties to perform municipal functions for cities under contracts with them.

TABLE 9

TRANSFERS OF FUNCTIONS TO CALIFORNIA COUNTIES
LOCATED IN METROPOLITAN AREAS

County*	Number of cities within the county	Total number of instances of functional transfers	Number of types of functional transfers
Alameda*.........	11	34	5
Contra Costa.......	11	32	6
Fresno*............	15	45	5
Los Angeles*.......	46	412	16
Marin.............	9	11	3
Orange............	15	44	5
Riverside*.........	12	82	10
Sacramento*.......	5	38	11
San Bernardino*....	10	83	9
San Diego*.........	9	67	10
San Joaquin*.......	5	28	8
San Mateo.........	13	103	12
Santa Clara*.......	13	43	5
Solano............	7	41	8

Note: An asterisk (*) indicates that the county contains a central city of a metropolitan area. San Francisco is excluded because it is both a city and a county.

Source: County Supervisors Association of California, *County-City Functional Consolidation in California* (Sacramento: 1956). The material in the table is based on a specially prepared tabulation made before the release of the final report, and is therefore preliminary. Appreciation is expressed to William R. MacDougall, the Association's general manager, for his courtesy in making the advance data available.

Two other legal authorizations, one adopted and the other pending, are potential contributors to the urban county movement in California. The first is the county service area law, adopted in 1953. This legislation recognizes the responsibility of counties to provide intensified services in unincorporated urban areas and provides a method for people in such areas to pay for them. It authorizes the county governing body to establish areas in which a special, local tax is levied to finance one or more extended services supplied by the county government.

The second potential contributor to the urban county development is a proposed constitutional amendment to be submitted to the voters of

California in November, 1956. It authorizes any county to provide in its charter for establishment of boroughs for all or any part of its unincorporated territory. If specified in the charter, boroughs can perform county functions, cooperate with cities and, with other boroughs or cities, jointly exercise powers granted to county and city governments. As is true of the county service area law, the proposed constitutional amendment grants to county governments the right to create tax differential zones. The amendment has great possible significance for the further development of the urban county idea.

The Growth of Central Management

In addition to the extensive legal grants, another major factor has facilitated the evolution of many California counties into urban governments. The state is easily one of the leaders in the development of central management in counties.[7] Three of its counties, all in metropolitan areas, have substantially reorganized their structural arrangements and have centered responsibility for administrative operations in a county manager. Sixteen others of the total of fifty-seven counties and one city-county, although most have not completed large-scale structural renovation, have established the post of chief administrative officer. The person who holds this position serves as an agent of the county governing body in coordinating and overseeing county governmental activities. The employment of complete or partial central management in numerous California counties has had two beneficial effects on the urban county trend. It has increased public confidence in the quality of county governmental performance, thus enlarging public willingness to have functions given over to counties. And it has strengthened the ability of county governments to undertake a larger number or more intensified activities, including those transferred from other units.

An Urban County Reversal

Proposals and adoptions to transform county governments in numerous metropolitan areas into metropolitan units are growing in frequency, but some counter actions are also evident. An outstanding example of

[7] A complete listing of the counties and the dates of adoption are contained in Winston W. Crouch and others, *California Government and Politics* (Englewood Cliffs: Prentice-Hall, 1956), ch. 12.

adoption of the opposing viewpoint is the Plan of Improvement for Atlanta and Fulton County, which went into effect in January, 1952. The plan provided for the annexation of eighty-two square miles to Atlanta, supplied a procedure for future annexations to the city by judicial determination, reallocated functions between the city and the county, and largely excluded the county government from performing municipal functions.[8] Fire protection, garbage collection, parks and recreation, sewerage, water and police activities were merged under the city government. In police work, for example, the county law enforcement department was made part of the city police department; the county's crime laboratory, police records and patrol cars became city property, and the county had to contract with the city for police protection in unincorporated areas. Under the plan, the Fulton County government continued to have exclusive jurisdiction over welfare activities throughout the county, and all public health work became its province.

Functional Transfers and Joint Efforts: An Appraisal

Functional transfers and joint efforts are increasing in number, but generally they have been used in a fragmentary manner. The piecemeal practice, which is a simple and easy approach to a service or control need, does not result in the simultaneous disturbance of many governmental relationships, and it has encountered little resistance. But the manner in which functional transfers and joint efforts have been employed in most metropolitan areas constitutes too slow an approach in view of the magnitude of the general metropolitan problem. Although they usually represent governmental progress in metropolitan areas, their over-all benefits have been too limited.

The urban county idea—in terms of comprehensive transfers of functions to county governments—offers the greatest possibilities for transforming this approach into an effective metropolitan method. There are several reasons why the urban county concept is gaining support. First, the territories of most counties more closely approximate the limits of metropolitan areas than do the boundaries of other general local units. Second, county governments have been growing stronger, through state legislative authorizations to undertake additional functions and transfers of single functions. Third, converting county governments into metro-

---

[8] M. Clyde Hughes, "Annexation and Reallocation of Functions," *Public Management*, 34 (February, 1952), pp. 26–30.

politan units may be easier to accomplish and as satisfactory in results as attempting to create new general governments of metropolitan jurisdiction; moreover, reorganized county governments can represent a type of federation. Fourth, in many instances other metropolitan approaches have been rejected or have proved insufficient after becoming operative.

Practically all supporters of the urban county plan agree that its development must be preceded by major reorganization of county governmental structure and processes. Such reform is necessary to enable county governments to perform additional functions competently and to increase public confidence in their ability to assume greatly enlarged responsibilities. A number of improvements, including financial control and central purchasing, have been placed in operation in some counties since 1917, when H. S. Gilbertson called county governments in general "the dark continent of American politics." The typical county in a metropolitan area and elsewhere, however, is still a "headless wonder" —a loosely organized alliance of many independently elected administrative officials and autonomous and semi-autonomous boards, subject to only moderate direction and supervision by the county governing body. Major reorganization of county governments, moreover, depends upon obtaining amendments to long-existing provisions in many state constitutions and acquiring alterations in state laws.

In some areas a different kind of county governmental reorganization may also be a necessary condition to use of the urban county idea. The present basis of representation on the county governing body may need to be revised. Numerous residents of incorporated places in certain counties will demand increased representation on the county governing body before they will support an urban county plan. County legislative apportionment on a reasonable basis, in combination with reallocation of functions and substantial structural reorganization, can result in the establishment of urban counties that constitute a type of federation.

The territorial size of counties—one of the principal grounds of support for the urban county idea—is at the same time a major limitation on the applicability of the concept in some metropolitan areas. The urban county plan has its greatest potential usefulness in metropolitan areas whose limits largely parallel county boundaries. Most metropolitan areas still do not extend beyond a single county, but an important minority, including many of the more populous metropolitan sections, are intercounty, and some are interstate. Whether two or more counties situated in intercounty or interstate metropolitan areas can become urban counties and work out an adequate series of transfers and combined efforts among themselves is debatable. In any event, additional legal authorizations would be necessary in a number of states.

Piecemeal functional transfers and joint efforts should not be regarded as steps leading eventually to the emergence of the full-fledged urban county. As has been indicated, realization of the latter must be preceded by important legal changes that at least in some states may be difficult to obtain. Basically, therefore, widespread adoption of the urban county concept depends upon acceptance by the people and their state legislative representatives of a broader role and a new organizational pattern for counties in metropolitan areas.

6. Metropolitan Special Districts

The growth in use of metropolitan special districts, largely since World War I and especially since World War II, represents a very noticeable development in government. In 1955 alone, for example, at least six new metropolitan districts in five widely scattered areas either were established or began operations. Despite the expanding significance of this metropolitan method, no general investigation and evaluation of such districts were undertaken until recently.[1]

Each metropolitan special district performs one or a few urban functions and territorially includes in most instances the central city and an important part of the rest of the metropolitan area.[2] There are two types of metropolitan districts. The first consists of independent governmental units; they possess considerable administrative and fiscal autonomy. The second type is made up of dependent entities; they have one or more characteristics of independent units but lack sufficient administrative or fiscal independence or both to qualify in that category and are therefore adjuncts of state and local governments.

The present section focuses on metropolitan special districts that are separate governments. They are identified as "independent metropolitan districts." Those in the dependent classification are used for comparative purposes.

Reasons for Growth

Rejection of Other Methods

The major reasons that are prompting the continuing increase of independent metropolitan districts warrant consideration. One principal cause of their growth is the frequency with which the voters reject other metropolitan approaches. In a number of metropolitan areas, the district method has been adopted only after unsuccessful attempts have been made to gain city-county consolidation or federation, for example. In this sense, the special district is at times a last resort.

---

[1] This section draws extensively on John C. Bollens, *Special District Governments in the United States* (Berkeley: University of California Press, 1956).

[2] The qualification "in most instances" is necessary because a few of these districts do not have defined areas, or they have small territorial limits but nevertheless affect many metropolitan people in important ways.

Many Enabling Laws and Liberal Adoption Procedures

Two additional reasons, related in some cases to the first, are the greater availability and the comparatively liberal nature of legal provisions for establishing independent metropolitan districts. Usually a legal basis for a district can be obtained more easily and takes the form of a state law rather than a constitutional amendment. The latter, which may be difficult to acquire, is generally necessary in city-county consolidation and federation efforts. Many more legal authorizations exist to permit the creation of the districts than apply to most other metropolitan methods, and the total has increased constantly in recent years.

Numerous adoption procedures permit the establishment of districts through a single area-wide popular vote or through state legislation that does not involve direct approval of the electorate of the metropolitan area. In this century supporters of certain other metropolitan approaches customarily have encountered more severe requirements for adoption. Because of these reasons, creation of independent metropolitan districts has been undertaken in some areas without previous serious efforts to use another approach.

A Restricted and Supplementary Method

A fourth reason for the growth of the districts is that, as usually employed, they represent a less comprehensive approach than most other metropolitan methods. In contrast to consolidation, federation and large-scale annexation, the use of independent metropolitan districts has not involved the abolition or substantial modification of existing local governments. The lack of such effects has had wide appeal in numerous metropolitan areas. It has gained support for the district device particularly from certain local officials who regard other approaches as endangering their governmental positions, and from a number of private individuals and organizations that oppose elimination or major disruption of particular local governments.

The inadequacy in certain metropolitan areas of other approaches after their adoption constitutes a fifth reason for the increase in independent metropolitan districts. Usually such a situation develops out of a legal obstacle to area change under the existing system, either because no provision for the change exists, or because it is difficult. The reorganized area is thus unable to expand its boundaries at all or sufficiently to keep pace with metropolitan expansion. This inability is especially evident in metropolitan areas that have become intercounty or interstate. Consequently, the New York, Philadelphia, San Francisco-Oakland, and St. Louis metropolitan areas, among others, are using the district approach as a supplement to another, previously adopted metropolitan method.

Limited Perspective

As a sixth reason, independent metropolitan districts in some instances are the result of applying a limited view to the general metropolitan problem. In metropolitan areas one or a few deficiencies in services and regulation usually are more acute than others. Concern about a single shortcoming thus may develop among individuals and groups without regard to other difficulties that are merely different in degree of intensity. A single-function outlook, at times fostered by professional and lay functional specialists, thus contributes to the use of the district method.

Principal Characteristics

Functions

Although collectively independent metropolitan districts undertake a broad range of activities, individually they perform one or a few related functions. The functions that many districts carry out represent all that are specified in the legal authorizations. Several functions, however, are performed by many more districts than others. Easily the most prevalent are port facilities and sewage disposal. Also numerous are parks, water supply, housing and airports. Other services, provided less frequently, include air pollution control, bridge construction and maintenance, electricity, flood control, gas supply, public health, hospital facilities and care, insect pest control, ice, levee construction and maintenance, and libraries. Still other district activities are in the fields of port promotion, regional planning, slum clearance, streets, mass transit service, transit survey, transportation and freight terminals, tunnel construction and maintenance, urban redevelopment and watercourse improvement.

The most common combinations of functions are water supply and sewage, and port and airport facilities. Most district activities involve service rather than regulation. Independent metropolitan districts perform many functions important to metropolitan areas, but certain ones usually regarded as metropolitan in nature are completely absent—most notably fire protection and law enforcement. Functions of dependent metropolitan districts largely parallel those carried out by districts of the independent category.

Location, Organization and Finance

Independent metropolitan districts are widespread in location. They are active in more than one of every four metropolitan areas and are present in more than half of the states. They are particularly numerous in California, Illinois, Ohio and Texas, which have been experiencing rapid metropolitan growth. Although the districts are functioning in metropolitan areas of various sizes, their greatest concentration is in those of 500,000 or more population. It is not unknown for two or more independent metropolitan districts to be in operation in the same metropolitan area and to overlie substantially the same territory. The Chicago and the Toledo metropolitan areas and the Oakland portion of the San Francisco-Oakland area have three each. It is not extraordinary for both independent and dependent metropolitan districts to be functioning in the same metropolitan area; those of Boston and Los Angeles are examples.

Only about one of every five independent metropolitan districts has a governing body composed entirely of members directly elected by the district voters. Most others have appointed members, and a few of them have both appointed and ex-officio directors. The appointing authority may be a single person or a group, such as the county governing body, the governor, or a judge or members of a court serving a jurisdiction that includes the territory of the district. In some districts there is a joint appointing authority of a dual or triple nature involving different units, levels or branches of government. In dependent metropolitan districts the governing body membership is appointed by the controlling government. The fundamental test of whether a metropolitan special district is independent or dependent, however, is its degree of administrative and financial autonomy and not the method of selecting its governing body.

Most independent metropolitan districts rely heavily on service charges, sales, rents and tolls. Many do not possess the power of taxation. A large proportion can float long-term bonds, and in numerous instances such authority can be used by the governing body without referral of the matter to the district residents or property owners.

The selection of governing body members by an official or group whose constituency is wider than that of the metropolitan area, and issuance of bonds on the decision of the district directors, may make metropolitan districts remote from area residents. These two elements are present in many metropolitan districts; they are uniformly present in those that are interstate. Districts with such characteristics operate in local areas but are not truly local governments in terms of accountability and control.

Complexity

A considerable number of independent metropolitan districts have a complicated organization or governing body composition. Some districts consist of a stratification of governments within governments as major and subordinate parts of their organizational structure. In one portion of the Metropolitan Water District of Southern California, for example, a public utility district and two cities are part of an irrigation district which is in turn part of a county water authority which in turn is a constituent member of the metropolitan water district. More commonly, the complexity results from the method of selecting the district governing body. The Chicago Transit Authority is an illustration. Three of its members are appointed by the governor with the consent of the state senate and the approval of the mayor of Chicago; the remaining four are selected by the mayor with the consent of the city council and the approval of the governor. Complexity reduces the understanding and interest of people residing in metropolitan areas and makes meaningful accountability to them difficult if not impossible.

Metropolitan Special Districts: An Appraisal

In numerous areas independent metropolitan districts are the closest approximations to jurisdictions of metropolitan scope and powers that are in operation.[3] In no area, however, are they individually undertaking many diversified functions; instead they are separately dealing with only a portion of the total metropolitan problem. At present, therefore,

[3] Here, as throughout this section, the emphasis is on special districts possessing independent governmental status.

they are all limited governments that are metropolitan mainly in territorial extent.

During the recent period of growth, independent metropolitan districts have received increased criticism. There are three common specific charges. One is their remoteness from influence and control by the people they serve and affect. The second is the limitation on the kinds of activities they can undertake because of the required reliance on sources of financing other than taxes. The third is that they do not contribute adequately to intergovernmental cooperation and coordinated planning. These criticisms cannot validly be made about all independent metropolitan districts, but one or more of them are applicable to many of these units.

A more general point of censure is relevant to all independent metropolitan districts as now operating. It centers on their restricted functional nature. As presently used, the district approach lacks sufficient comprehensiveness to deal with the general metropolitan problem. Its limited functional nature leads to further proliferation of governmental units, to more widespread citizen confusion and to inadequate popular control of the governmental system. Moreover, in undertaking to solve one or a few critical difficulties, independent metropolitan districts divert interest away from more thorough efforts at reorganization. By alleviating an extremely pressing matter, they may tend to lull local residents into a false sense of satisfaction that the total metropolitan problem, which consists of many deficiencies, has been solved.

At the same time that criticisms of the present form of independent metropolitan districts have mounted, interest in revising the district approach has gained support. The more widely advocated line of reform calls for at least two types of provisions in new legal authorizations—usually state laws and interstate compacts—or their inclusion as amendments to existing authorizations. One proposal is to empower independent metropolitan districts to be multipurpose, thus in effect converting them into general governments of metropolitan scope. Another is to place them under local control and to broaden their means of financing. An additional possibility, which also seems advisable in order to avoid numerous single-purpose uses of multipurpose authorizations, is to limit the number of these governments that can be established in any one metropolitan area.

Experience with existing independent metropolitan districts seemingly indicates that such revisions might be acceptable to people in various metropolitan areas. In the past, public acceptance of the district idea has not appreciably lessened when a number of functions have been conferred upon particular types of independent metropolitan districts. In fact, a small number of them are currently organized in accordance with the reforms suggested, although no district has made substantial use of its broad grant of powers. The key point of strategy in gaining widespread acceptance of this revised form may well be for such a district initially to perform only a few functions, then gradually to make wider use of its authorized functions as the people express satisfaction in the quality of its past levels of performance.

A second line of reform that has been suggested is to convert many existing independent metropolitan districts into entities dependent on the state government or the county government. In general, this suggested reform seems to have less support than the one just discussed. Conversion to the status of an agency dependent on the state runs counter to the widespread desire for a metropolitan-controlled operation. Conversion to county-dependent status will be unacceptable in numerous metropolitan areas so long as the county governments are not substantially reorganized. Even then, such reform could be used effectively only in metropolitan areas that are not intercounty.

The first line of reform, calling for multipurpose independent district governments, could largely be accomplished through passage of new state laws and revision of existing legislation, and in some situations by legislatures entering into amended or new interstate compacts. The problem of state constitutional change encountered by many other metropolitan methods would be virtually nonexistent in setting up these district governments.

Adoption of this revised district form (which could, if desired, be organized to constitute a type of federation) thus depends upon state action and upon support by the people in metropolitan areas. If these two steps materialize, a much criticized governmental unit may well be changed into a comprehensive and more effective metropolitan structure.

TABLE 10
Independent Metropolitan Districts

District name*	Activities began	Area (square miles)	Functions currently performed	Governing bd. selection method†	Revenue sources‡
CALIFORNIA					
Alameda Co. Mosquito Abatement Dist. (Oakland)	1930	445	Insect pest contr.	A	GPS
Bay Area Air Pollution Con. Dist. (San Francisco)	1955	....	Air pollution contr.[1]	A	P
East Bay Mun. Utility Dist. (Oakland)	1929	215	Sewage disposal, water supply	E	PS
East Bay Regional Park Dist. (Oakland)	1934	....	Parks	E	PS
Golden Gate Bridge & Highway Dist. (San Francisco)	1928	10,000	Bridge constr. and maintenance	A	S
Metrop. Water Dist. of Southern California	1928	2,800	Water supply	A	PS
Sacramento-Yolo Mosquito Abatement Dist.	1947	2,013	Insect pest contr.	A	GP
Sacramento-Yolo Port Dist.	1947	1,200	Port facilities	A	PS
San Bernardino Valley Mun. Water Dist.	1954	223	Water supply[1]	E	AP
San Diego County Water Authority	1944	546	Water supply	A	GPS
Stockton Port Dist.	1932	....	Port facilities	A	GPS
COLORADO					
Moffat Tunnel Improvement Dist. (Denver)	1922	9,200	Tunnel constr. and maintenance, water supply	E	PS
CONNECTICUT					
Metropolitan Dist. (Hartford)	1930	134	Regional planning, sewage disposal, water supply	A	AST
FLORIDA					
Pinellas Co. Anti-Mosquito Dist. (St. Petersburg)	1930	270	Insect pest contr.	E	GP
GEORGIA					
Fulton-DeKalb Hosp. Authority (Atlanta)[2]	1946	820	Hospital	A	PS
Savannah Dist. Authority	1951	441	Port facilities	A	ApS
ILLINOIS					
Chicago Regional Port Dist.	1955	....	Port facilities	A	S
Chicago Transit Authority	1947	730	Mass transit service	A	GS
Greater Peoria Airport Authority	1950	96	Airport operation	A	GP
Greater Peoria Sanitary & Sewage Disposal Dist.	1927	32	Sewage disposal	A	APS
Metrop. Sanitary Dist. of Greater Chicago	1889	490	Sewage disposal	E	P
Pleasure Driveway and Park Dist. (Peoria)	1894	39	Parks	E	ADPS
Springfield Sanitary Dist.[2]	1924	37	Sewage disposal	A	APS
INDIANA					
Marion Co. Health & Hosp. Corp. (Indianapolis)[2]	1954	402	Health, hospitals	A	GPS

Independent metropolitan districts on which current data were not available when the table was compiled are Dallas City and County Levee Improvement District, Dallas County Flood Control District, Housing Authority of the City of Dallas, Sacramento Municipal Utility District and Tri-State Airport Authority (Huntington, West Virginia).

Source of table: John C. Bollens, "Metropolitan Special Districts," *Municipal Year Book 1956* (Chicago: International City Managers' Association, 1956). The material is reproduced with the express permission of the publisher.

* *District Name:* The metropolitan central city (or the more populous one when there are two) within the district is designated in parentheses when it is not identifiable from the name of the district. Interstate districts are listed under the state in which the most populous central city is located and are indicated by a star (*).

† *Governing Board—Selection Method:* A, appointed by governor, county governing body or other public officials; E, elected by people residing within the district; Ex, members serve ex officio from the state government or from other local governments in the district.

‡ *Revenue Sources:* A, special assessments; Ap, appropriations from member units (in some instances on the basis of proportionate use of district facilities) of the district or from contracting units; D, donations and gifts; P, local property taxes; R, royalties; S, service charges, sales, rents and tolls; T, tax on member units within the district.

[1] Indicates functions the district intends to provide; the district is now active and in the planning or construction stage.

[2] Information gathered in 1955; data on all other districts collected in 1956.

TABLE 10—*Continued*

District name*	Activities began	Area (square miles)	Functions currently performed	Governing bd. selection method†	Revenue sources‡
LOUISIANA					
Orleans Levee Dist. (New Orleans).............	1890	364	Airport operation, levee constr. and maintenance, parks, streets	AEx	APRS
MAINE					
Maine Port Authority (Portland)...............	1923	....	Port facilities	A	GDS
MASSACHUSETTS					
Boston Metropolitan Dist....................	1929	129	Mass transit service[3]	A	Ap
Metropolitan Transit Authority (Boston)........	1947	129	Mass transit service	A	S
MICHIGAN					
Huron-Clinton Metrop. Authority (Detroit)......	1941	3,252	Parks	A	P
MINNESOTA					
Minneapolis-St. Paul Metrop. Airports Commn...	1943	2,000	Airport operation	AEx	GPS
Minneapolis-St. Paul Sanitary Dist.............	1933	109	Sewage disposal	AEx	PS
MISSOURI					
Bi-State Development Dist. (St. Louis)*........	1949	2,911	Port facil., regional planning	A	GS
Metrop. St. Louis Sewer Dist..................	1954	222	Sewage disposal	A	AGPS
NEBRASKA					
Metrop. Utilities Dist. of Omaha..............	1912	60	Gas supply, ice, water supply	E	AS
Omaha Public Power Dist.....................	1946	2,500	Electricity	E	S
Sanitary Dist. No. 1 of Lancaster Co. (Lincoln)..	1891	52	Flood control, sewage disposal	E	APS
NEW JERSEY					
Passaic Valley Sewage Dist. (Newark)..........	1902	100	Sewage disposal	A	Ap
NEW YORK					
Albany Port Dist...........................	1930	35	Port facilities	A	GS
Port of New York Authority*.................	1921	1,500	Airport operation, bridge constr. and maintenance, port facil., transp. and freight term., tunnel constr. and maintenance	A	GS
OHIO					
Akron Metrop. Housing Authority.............	1938	408	Housing	A	GS
Akron Metrop. Park Dist.[2]..................	1924	600	Parks	A	APS
Cleveland Metrop. Housing Authority..........	1933	455	Housing, slum clearance	A	GS
Cleveland Metrop. Park Dist..................	1917	488	Parks	A	GPS
Columbus Metrop. Housing Authority..........	1934	552	Housing	A	GS
Columbus & Franklin Co. Metrop. Park Dist.....	1947	....	Parks	A	PS
Hamilton Co. Park Dist. (Cincinnati)...........	1930	408	Parks	A	APS
Hamilton Co. Library Dist. (Cincinnati)........	1933	415	Library	A	......
Toledo Area Sanitary Dist....................	1946	153	Insect pest contr.	A	A
Toledo-Lucas Co. Port Authority..............	1956	307	Port facilities	A	PS
Toledo Metrop. Housing Authority.............	1933	334	Housing	A	S

[3] The sole function of this district is to raise money on its bonds, the money being used to equip and maintain the Metropolitan Transit Authority (Boston).

TABLE 10—*Continued*

District name*	Activities began	Area (square miles)	Functions currently performed	Governing bd. selection method†	Revenue sources‡
OREGON					
Port of Portland	1891	218	Airport operation, port facilities, watercourse improv.	A	GPS
PENNSYLVANIA					
Delaware River Port Authority (Philadelphia)*	1952	4,582	Bridge constr. and maintenance, port facil., transit survey	AEx	S
SOUTH CAROLINA					
Greater Greenville Sewer Dist.	1926	40	Sewage disposal, water supply	A	P
TENNESSEE					
Memphis Housing Authority	1938	121	Housing	A	GS
TEXAS					
Harris Co.-Houston Ship Channel Navigation Dist.	1911	1,747	Port facilities	A	PS
Housing Authority of Fort Worth[2]	1938		Housing	A	GS
Housing Authority of San Antonio	1937	1,247	Housing	A	GS
Nueces Co. Navigation Dist. No. 1 (Corpus Christi)[2]	1926	838	Port facilities	A	S
Tarrant Co. Water Control & Improvement Dist. No. 1 (Fort Worth)	1924	201	Water supply	E	P
UTAH					
Central Weber Sewer Improvement Dist. (Ogden)	1953	45	Sewage disposal[1]	A	APS
Weber Basin Water Conservancy Dist. (Ogden)[2]	1950	2,000	Water supply	A	P
VIRGINIA					
Hampton Roads Sanitation Dist. (Norfolk)	1947	1,160	Sewage disposal	A	GS
WASHINGTON					
Metrop. Park Dist. of Tacoma	1907	69	Parks	E	ADPS
Port of Seattle	1913	2,298	Airport operation, port facilities	E	GPS
Port of Tacoma[2]	1918	1,676	Airport operation, port facilities	E	PS
WISCONSIN					
Housing Authority of Milwaukee	1944	72	Housing, urban redevel.	A	GS
Green Bay Metropolitan Sewerage Dist.	1932	26	Sewage disposal	A	AGPS
Madison Metropolitan Sewerage Dist.	1930	85	Sewage disposal	A	APS
Metropolitan Sewerage Dist. (Milwaukee)	1913	152	Sewage disposal, watercourse improv.	A	PS

Part Three

THE RESPONSIBILITIES OF THE STATES

A Suggested Program for the States

Five basic and closely related steps are suggested for the consideration of state governments as means of obtaining appropriate organization and development in metropolitan areas:

1. Establish legal authorizations for the creation of general metropolitan units that can be adequate in functions, financing ability, and structure. These units may be of one or more of three types: multipurpose metropolitan district, federation, and urban county. (Pages 132–36.)

2. Determine which method is preferable for putting the selected type or types of unit into effect: legislative action, local voter decision, or administrative or judicial determination. (Pages 136–38.)

3. Provide suitable legal provisions relating to two supplementary procedures: annexation and inter-local agreements. (Pages 138–39.)

4. Appraise the adequacy of local governments in terms of area, financial ability, administrative organization, administrative methods, and amount of discretion in the exercise of powers. Make necessary changes in accordance with the results of the appraisal. (Pages 140–44.)

5. Create or adapt an agency (1) to aid in determining the present and changing needs of metropolitan and non-metropolitan areas in the state and (2) to analyze the effects in such areas of current and contemplated policies of national, state and local governments and major private organizations. (Pages 144–47.)

PART THREE

The Responsibilities of the States

THE metropolitan problem unquestionably is one of the most critical domestic difficulties facing an increasingly urban United States. It presents a major challenge to the ingenuity of the people of our democratic society. Practically nowhere has a comprehensive solution been put into operation, and the problem is becoming greater as more and more people become residents of metropolitan areas. By 1950 almost three-fifths of the nation's population lived in such areas. The trend is continuing as this decade advances. Metropolitan areas are growing spectacularly. Their local governments are increasingly incapable of satisfying public needs that extend beyond individual governmental boundaries or range of authorized functions. Many current and contemplated actions of public and private organizations that affect metropolitan area residents are being undertaken in an uncoordinated manner.

The results of continuing population growth, inadequate governmental machinery, and unrelated and sometimes conflicting governmental and private programs of national, state and local extent are readily apparent. In many localities an occasional glance at the newspapers can reveal some of the most obvious deficiencies—deficiencies that affect people in both metropolitan and non-metropolitan areas. We have become very familiar with dwindling water supplies and disintegrated means of distribution, water and air pollution, contradictory and uneconomic land-use policies, and large-scale defects in various forms of transportation. Common also are archaic methods of sewage disposal, excessive noise, dirt and congestion, uneven provision of health and other protective services, and disruption of the metropolitan economy by unrelated decisions on industrial and commercial locations. Less publicized but highly important are the inconveniences and excessive costs of these shortcomings, the inequalities imposed upon various sections of metropolitan areas in financing services, and the impotence and frustration of attempts at citizen control.

Recent Growth of Interest

Concern on the part of numerous governments and private organizations—national, state and local—over the seriousness and significance of the metropolitan problem is now growing rapidly. If it continues to grow, the prospects must be judged favorable for substantial improvement of the inadequate current record of metropolitan accomplishments. A sampling of recent and present developments indicates how widespread and intensive interest has become.

Accelerated interest of national scope is very noticeable, and part of it involves governments directly. In January, 1955, the *Economic Report of the President* drew attention to the critical nature of specific weaknesses in metropolitan areas and called upon the states to study the problems so that "area-wide transit systems, sanitation systems, water supplies, or educational facilities may be provided with maximum returns from public funds expended." In June the national Commission on Intergovernmental Relations issued its *Report*. "It is clearly the responsibility of the States," the Commission noted, "to assume leadership in seeking solutions for the problems of metropolitan government."[1] In August the Governors' Conference adopted a resolution directing the Council of State Governments to make a general study of the metropolitan problem and to formulate suggestions designed to improve the situation. The present study is the result of that resolution.

Meanwhile, national associations of private citizens and public officials have increased their attention to the metropolitan problem. The recently organized Government Affairs Foundation is developing methods of cooperation between groups and individuals who want to attack the difficulties. It has completed a comprehensive bibliography on metropolitan communities that emphasizes the roles of government and politics, and an analytical digest of metropolitan surveys undertaken since 1924. Three other national organizations, in particular, moved forward with programs in this field in 1955. At its annual conference the American Municipal Association adopted a resolution to create a special committee. The committee is charged with evaluating research and experimentation under way and reporting solutions that offer the most efficient governmental organization of metropolitan areas while guaranteeing maximum citizen participation. The American Political

---

[1] *Economic Report of the President* (Washington: Government Printing Office, 1955), p. 64; Commission on Intergovernmental Relations, *Report* (Washington: 1955), p. 52.

Science Association received a foundation grant to undertake metropolitan research. The American Bar Association authorized its Section of Municipal Law to form a committee to cooperate with other interested groups. Other national associations, including the National Municipal League, the American Society for Public Administration, and various planning and public health organizations, are giving much attention to the subject in their publications and meetings.

In April, 1956, twenty agencies, most of them nation-wide in their membership, held the first national conference on metropolitan problems. At the conclusion of the meetings held for four days at East Lansing, Michigan, it was decided to establish a continuing national conference. The conference was authorized to facilitate cooperation among organizations and individuals concerned with the metropolitan problem.

Activity by individual state governments also is growing. Metropolitan studies authorized by the legislatures and undertaken by interim committees and legislative councils are in progress in California, Connecticut, Illinois, Ohio, Oregon, Utah, Wisconsin and other states. Three examples will indicate the comprehensiveness of the assignments. The Northeastern Illinois Metropolitan Area Local Governmental Services Commission is studying service problems relating to public health, safety and welfare in the Chicago area. The Utah Local Government Survey Commission is investigating the functions and services of local governments and the advisability of a metropolitan governmental organization. In Ohio the Legislative Service Commission is analyzing the laws that pertain to government in the metropolitan areas of the state.

Numerous public and private study groups are making broad investigations in various metropolitan areas. For example, the Harris County Home Rule Commission, authorized by the Texas legislature, is examining the situation in the Houston area and will make recommendations to the legislature in 1957. Official metropolitan area committees advisory to the city and county governments are functioning in the Fresno and Sacramento areas, and studies are about to begin. A comprehensive analysis of the St. Louis area is starting under the sponsorship of Washington and St. Louis universities. The Cleveland Metropolitan Services Commission, formed by agreement of public officials and political leaders in Cuyahoga County and the Citizens' League of Cleveland, is active in initiating a detailed fact-finding project. The Municipal League of Seattle and King County is moving ahead with the development of a solution to alleviate the local metropolitan problem. Many other organizations are at work under public and private auspices, analyzing the applicability of particular approaches to the difficulties of their specific areas.

Recommendations and studies by various governments and private organizations thus demonstrate the expanding interest and concern over the metropolitan problem. Growing advocacy of reform in particular areas is especially encouraging. All of these activities represent important steps. But more is needed than general and local interest, study and support.

Although the roles of local governments and the national government are indispensable, the states are the key to solving the complex difficulties that make up the general metropolitan problem. To achieve adequate results the state governments—the legislative and executive branches and the people—need to exert positive, comprehensive and sustained leadership in solving the problem and keeping it solved.

The states should assume three responsibilities in particular: (1) adoption of legal provisions authorizing the establishment of general metropolitan units; (2) appraisal of the adequacy of local governments; and (3) creation of continuing agencies to analyze and recommend on the needs and developments of metropolitan and non-metropolitan areas.

Authorizing General Metropolitan Units

The states should establish legal authorizations for the creation of general metropolitan units that will be adequate in functions, financing ability and structure. In some states this can be accomplished through improvement of existing state laws and constitutional provisions; in others, where no legal provisions exist, additions to the laws and constitutions rather than revisions of them will be needed. In an increasing number of states, interstate legal arrangements will be required. In all such authorizations—revised and new state laws, constitutional provisions and interstate compacts—the states occupy the central position.[2]

Three principles are advisable as guides in revising or preparing legal authorizations.

[2] In several states, where certain activities in metropolitan areas have important impact across national boundaries, international agreements between the national governments of the United States and Canada or Mexico may be required. They will be less numerous, however, than the other forms of legal authority.

The Responsibilities of the States

The first is that the metropolitan units should be permitted to exercise a range of functions sufficient to eliminate, or reduce noticeably, service and regulatory deficiencies that are area-wide or present in more than one locality of the area. The scope of the functions granted to the units should be equal to the extent of the needs. The units should be endowed with functions to be exercised throughout their entire areas, as well as functions that are more than local but less than area-wide and that are not assigned to the municipal or county units operating within their boundaries. Moreover, the authorizations should contain a procedure or permission for the future reallocation of functions among the directly affected governments.

The second principle is that the metropolitan units be given a broad and equitable basis for financing, including the powers to levy taxes, issue bonds and make service charges. They should possess such powers so that they can undertake activities that are metropolitan and more than local and that cannot be financed on a self-supporting basis limited to service charges and revenue bonds. It may be essential to grant the units the right to levy taxes and assessments at different rates in various parts of their areas when services are not provided uniformly.

Third, the metropolitan units should be constructed in most instances so that they are directly responsible to, and controlled by, the people of the metropolitan areas in which they operate. The members of their governing bodies should be either elected by the metropolitan area residents or appointed by the governing bodies of the member local governments. The former arrangement makes public accountability and control more direct; the latter may facilitate understanding and cooperation between the metropolitan and local levels of government. The state-wide importance of the activities of some metropolitan units may make it desirable to have certain members of their governing bodies appointed by the governor.

No one uniform type of general metropolitan unit can be prescribed for all metropolitan areas. Three types, however, generally have the greatest merit—the multipurpose metropolitan district, the federation arrangement, and the comprehensive urban county form. The basic features of all three are the establishment of a metropolitan level of government to assume area-wide and more than local functions and the retention of local governments to perform strictly local activities. They create a metropolitan mechanism capable of fulfilling unmet needs, while preserving local units for the important purposes of handling a number of public matters and providing channels for close and significant citizen participation.

There is growing interest in many metropolitan areas in these types of general units. Paralleling and related to growing advocacy of them is increased opposition to proposals requiring the creation of metropolitan governments to replace all general local governments. The use of the multipurpose district or the federation or the urban county type can result in establishment of adequate general metropolitan units without obliterating strictly local governments, which can properly perform important roles in metropolitan areas. Any one of the three types can provide for representation of local areas on the metropolitan governing body.

The desirability of organization that provides for creation of a metropolitan unit and retention of a local level of government does not mean that it is advisable to preserve all existing local governments in every metropolitan area. Some local units, for example, may have highly artificial territorial limits and may be too small for efficient and economic operation. But, although local governments may be regrouped, the result should be a strengthening of the local level of government.

All three types of preferred general metropolitan units have their appropriate uses. Although one may be preferable to the others in particular situations, none stands out as universally superior. The establishment of multipurpose metropolitan districts usually involves the fewest legal changes, especially in state constitutions. This is because major structural or functional reorganization of county governments, or elimination of them, does not necessarily have to accompany the creation of such districts. Usually, state laws can form the legal basis of districts whose territory lies in one county or in more than one county in one state, and interstate compacts can be the foundation of those that are interstate.

No metropolitan district is performing numerous and diverse functions in any metropolitan area in the United States today. Independent and dependent metropolitan districts of limited purpose are in operation in a number of intercounty metropolitan areas and in a more limited number of interstate metropolitan areas. Several of them possess a sufficiently broad range of powers to approximate multipurpose districts, but they do not use more than a few of the many functions granted to them.

The greater legal facility with which multipurpose districts may be established, in comparison with urban county or federation plans, can

The Responsibilities of the States

be overvalued. A more basic consideration is whether in a particular area either the reform or abolition of county government is necessary to the construction of a sound system of metropolitan and local levels of government. In interstate metropolitan areas, moreover, the judgment that it is legally easier to create multipurpose metropolitan districts can be deceptive. In establishing such governments, the participating states should review some of their other laws and constitutional sections (such as over-all tax limits and state regulation of specific activities) that would affect the operations of the districts. The pertinent legal provisions of the participating states would have to be made reasonably uniform in their application to the districts if these governments were to function effectively.[3]

Federation involves comprehensive governmental reorganization since it adds a general metropolitan unit, either eliminates one or more county governments or reduces their powers, and decreases the functions of municipalities. In many states such metropolitan area reform would require amendment of the constitution. Federation proposals generally have stipulated that the limits of the metropolitan unit would parallel the boundaries of a county government to be replaced. In a sense, then, such a proposal usually has represented the actual reorganization of the county governmental area but not literally the reorganization of the county government itself, because the latter would cease to exist.

Federation plans occasionally have been cast in an intercounty framework, but in each instance the existing county governments that would have been replaced were relatively unimportant, and no state constitutions guaranteed their continued existence. Whether counties are performing major functions, and whether their existence is based on state laws or constitutional provisions, may be decisive factors in determining whether to use federation in some intercounty metropolitan areas. Although past federation proposals have called for the abolition of at least one county government in each area involved, counties can be retained in federated arrangements. They possibly should be retained in certain intercounty federations to carry out functions that are less than area-wide but more than local.

No legal arrangements now exist between states to permit adoption of federation in interstate metropolitan areas. If such arrangements are adopted, they should guarantee to the participating states the retention

[3] The need for examining and probably adjusting other legislative and constitutional provisions applies equally to the establishment of interstate federated governments.

of their respective territories that are within the federation. Otherwise, interstate federation might be regarded as involving the abdication of area by one state to another.

The urban county approach is the only one of the three types in which existing governments always would be transformed into metropolitan units. This may be an advantage in cases in which legislatures and the public would more readily accept the revision of already established governments—counties—in preference to creation of new governments. On the other hand, it may be a disadvantage if renovation of operating governments promises to be more difficult than establishment of new ones. In many instances, the structural changes considered necessary for conversion of counties into effective metropolitan units would have to be authorized in state constitutional provisions; at present most constitutions do not contain such provisions. Where adopted, the urban county idea will have its greatest usefulness in one-county metropolitan areas. In metropolitan areas that are intercounty or interstate it is questionable whether two (and in some cases more) adjacent counties could work out a series of cooperative agreements sufficient in total to be adequate general metropolitan arrangements.

Methods of Adoption

The methods used for placing any of the three preferred types of general metropolitan units into effect will differ among the states. In some states the method selected will be for the legislature, on the basis of detailed study and analysis, to pass suitable legislation making a metropolitan unit operative. A number of metropolitan reorganizations, including city-county consolidations and large-scale annexations, were activated through passage of state laws. Although many of these laws stipulating comprehensive area reform were enacted in the last century, the necessary authority currently rests with some state legislatures if they wish to exercise it.

In various states—possibly many—the method favored will be to make adoption a matter of local determination. Where this is employed, it is fundamental that there be an equitable voting procedure. Consent of the majority of the participating voters is a widely accepted standard in the process of local determination. The difficult task, however, is deciding whether one, two or multiple majorities shall be required. In some states a requirement of a single over-all vote of the people in a metropolitan area—used successfully in 1947 in connection with the Baton Rouge–East Baton Rouge Parish consolidation plan—will be favored. In other states two or more electoral areas will be stipulated. This may involve the combining of several governmental areas for the purpose of the election, along the lines of the legal provisions used in the St. Louis consolidation effort of 1926 and in school district consolidation proposals in a number of states beginning in the 1940's.

It seems inadvisable to have adoption depend on separate approval by a majority of the voters of each existing local government when numerous local units are involved, or to set up electoral areas so that local governments collectively containing a small portion of the total metropolitan population possess the power to block acceptance of a proposal. Likewise it seems inadvisable to grant the right of exclusive judgment on a proposition to the electorate or the governing body of one government. In brief, the requirement should apply the concept of metropolitan home rule instead of strictly local home rule. In working out an electoral formula, it should be kept in mind that the number and nature of the required majorities have contributed to the poor record of voter adoptions of metropolitan propositions.

Some states may find a third method of adopting any of the three types of general metropolitan units desirable. It is similar to that of the Virginia annexation courts and the municipal board of Ontario Province, though broader in scope. This method, as yet unused in any state, would permit a state administrative tribunal possessing quasi-judicial powers or, alternatively, judges constituting a special court, to put a metropolitan unit into effect upon determining the need and learning the desires of the people of a metropolitan area.

In making a choice between the alternatives, the interested states would need to decide whether this important assignment represented too heavy a burden on judges and too much a diversion from their main duties, and whether administrative tribunals composed of specially trained persons would do a superior job. Regardless of which body is selected, the administrative tribunal or the special court would need to be aided by professional research analysts, and it should be given the right to initiate actions (a right that should also be granted to local governments) and to call its own witnesses. Interest has grown recently in this method of adoption because of increased published writings and discussion about annexation courts in Virginia and because of extensive publicity given the Toronto area federation plan proposed by the municipal board of Ontario and enacted by the provincial legislature.

Two other procedures—annexation and inter-local agreements—should be available for supplementary use after general metropolitan units become operative. Annexation is important to (1) general metropolitan units as the metropolitan areas in which they function grow in size, (2) local governments operating within general metropolitan units that contain unincorporated territory, and (3) urban areas approaching metropolitan status as a means of keeping their governmental systems comprehensible and effective. The annexation procedure used by metropolitan units would have to differ from that available to local governments in metropolitan and non-metropolitan areas, if the latter did not permit cross-county annexations and inclusion of incorporated places.

Adequate use of the annexation device depends in large part upon constructive revision of many state laws so that areas under consideration for annexation cannot control initiation of action and the final decision. The right to annex across county lines also is needed. Moreover, the effectiveness of the annexation process—especially in unincorporated sections within general metropolitan units and in urban areas starting to develop metropolitan conditions—depends partially upon making many incorporation provisions more difficult. Numerous states should review their incorporation laws to determine if the minimum population required for incorporation is too low, thus leading to a proliferation of small and frequently uneconomic municipalities in areas that are, or seemingly soon will be, metropolitan.

Authorizations for inter-local cooperative agreements similarly represent a worth-while supplement.[4] The procedure is important to local governments operating within general metropolitan units unless the latter have broad grants of powers in inter-local as well as area-wide matters. It also is very valuable to local governments functioning in urban areas that are nearing metropolitan status. It may be useful to general metropolitan units in certain of their relations with adjoining non-metropolitan as well as adjacent metropolitan areas. Proposed state laws to

---

[4] For a suggested act conferring comprehensive authorization in this field, see Council of State Governments, Drafting Committee of State Officials, *Suggested State Legislation: Program for 1956* (Chicago: 1955), pp. 24–30. The proposal permits inter-local agreements across state lines as well as within the boundaries of a single state. Those in the former category are specifically given the status of interstate compacts.

The Responsibilities of the States

authorize the completion of inter-local agreements can be stated in broad functional terms, but it may be crucial to their legislative adoption and to their successful use locally that they provide specific means of financing the arrangements.

Devices of Secondary Importance

Two other approaches to the metropolitan problem may be desirable in a limited number of areas. City-county consolidation or large-scale annexation may be preferred when a particular metropolitan area encompasses a relatively small amount of territory and contains very few incorporated places. Under these conditions a consolidated city-county would more closely approximate the metropolitan limits unless the state law permitted annexation of incorporated areas.

Even when the conditions of relatively small size and comparatively few incorporated places are present, the establishment of sub-areas within the jurisdiction of the consolidated government or the substantially enlarged city should accompany the use of city-county consolidation and large-scale annexation. Such sub-areas can appropriately serve as valuable channels through which neighborhood and local community ideas and requests, as well as reactions to current and contemplated policies, can be transmitted. The use of neighborhood and community councils in Kansas City, Missouri, and of administrative centers in Los Angeles, Los Angeles County and New York City are developments that deserve consideration elsewhere in the establishment of sub-areas. Another possibility meriting study is the nomination or election of the governing body members from sub-areas of the city-county or city.

City-county consolidation and large-scale annexation, however, generally are metropolitan methods of secondary importance. The establishment of sub-areas when these methods are used will partially eliminate one of the strongest objections to them—that they create a large government to the exclusion of more localized centers for citizen support and opposition. Such sub-areas, however, will not be real local governmental units that determine the level of local services and provide them directly to people in the individual localities. In other words, the proposed sub-areas in consolidated governments and in large-scale annexation arrangements are not the equivalent of local governments that function as important parts of multipurpose districts, federations or comprehensive urban counties.

It is worth emphasizing again that other currently used approaches are insufficient to meet the magnitude of the difficulties facing most metropolitan areas. As indicated earlier, two of them—transfers of functions, and independent and dependent metropolitan districts of limited purposes—can be converted through changes in legal authorizations into two of the most advantageous metropolitan methods: the comprehensive form of the urban county idea and the multipurpose metropolitan district. As presently constituted, however, piecemeal transfers and limited-purpose metropolitan districts usually are inadequate. Their restricted actions may in fact have serious detrimental effects. They may divert attention, at least temporarily, from comprehensive methods of attacking the general metropolitan problem, which characteristically involves many shortcomings and numerous governments. They also may further complicate the already involved intergovernmental relationships in metropolitan areas.

City-county separation, the last of the approaches now in use, is without value as a long-range, generally applicable method of dealing with the metropolitan problem. It conceivably has current usefulness in a very limited number of instances, under highly unusual circumstances—when the county in which a central city is located is extraordinarily large and contains a sizable amount of non-metropolitan territory that evidently will not become metropolitan in the future. Even under these circumstances, use of the device can be significant only if the city, in separating, gains all the territory that is currently metropolitan and obtains a liberal annexation procedure. Moreover, the combination of territorial enlargement and separation of the central city will severely reduce the resources of the remaining county and consequently may appreciably weaken its ability to be an adequate unit of government, thus necessitating its consolidation with an adjacent county. The latter action may or may not improve the possibilities of satisfying the public needs of residents of the county remaining after separation. In the occasional situations in which city-county separation might be employed, it is advisable to establish sub-areas within the enlarged, separated city.

Appraising Local Governments

It is recommended that the states undertake another responsibility that is important in solving the metropolitan problem—appraising the adequacy of their present systems of local government. These evalua-

The Responsibilities of the States

tions are essential for all types of metropolitan organizations that retain local governments to undertake specific duties. They are also necessary to determine the changes that are needed in certain local governments, such as counties in some metropolitan areas, in order to transform them into effective general metropolitan units. Moreover they are important in local areas that are not metropolitan.

Although the details will differ, it will be found in many states that metropolitan as well as non-metropolitan areas lack adequate systems of local government. Cities and other local governments have made much progress during the present century, most notably in organization and in internal operations, but numerous and extensive changes still are necessary. Metropolitan areas in particular have an unsatisfactory pattern—a large number of units that represent an illogical patchwork of suppliers of services and regulation. A clear indication of the deficiency of the governmental system of many metropolitan areas is the rapid and continuing rise of non-school special districts.[5] From 1942 to 1952 these districts, many of which are small and costly, grew approximately 48 per cent in number throughout the United States.

In strengthening their local governments the states should seek to develop units that can efficiently perform their functions and that can provide opportunities for broad citizen participation in local affairs.

Local government systems have several major shortcomings that need to be rectified to make them effective performers of essential functions and effective members of metropolitan units. These shortcomings include inadequacies in area, financial ability, administrative organization, administrative methods, and amount of discretion in the exercise of their powers. Not all of these defects are present in every state, nor are they uniform in intensity where they exist. They are sufficiently frequent, however, to be characterized as general weaknesses.

An excessive number of local governments exists, and many of them are too small in area. They are not large enough to perform local functions efficiently and economically and, for practically all functions, they are unable to meet modern standards of service. Some of them are largely relics of a former period of importance and have little present-day vitality. Others are expedients that have been established to supplement existing local units. It is suggested that the states undertake or encour-

---

[5] See John C. Bollens, *Special District Governments in the United States* (Berkeley: University of California Press, 1956), chapters 1 and 8, for an analysis of how special districts are symptomatic of shortcomings in other governments.

age the abolition of some of them, such as townships in some states, the consolidation of certain units—cities, towns, villages, and boroughs—with other incorporated places, and the merger of numerous limited-purpose districts with general local governments.

The example of the recent extensive consolidation of school districts, stimulated in part by state grants and other state action, needs to be applied to a major portion of the pattern of local government.[6] Providing an adequate area is a fundamental step in strengthening the local government system. Without it the correction of many other inadequacies will have unsatisfactory results.

Many local governments have insufficient financial ability. In many instances it will continue to be insufficient even after the suggested area reorganizations occur, unless the states remedy the difficulties. The needs will vary within metropolitan organizations according to the extent and nature of the functions assigned to local governments. Adequate financing ability, however, is basic to both metropolitan and local units.

The financing ability of local governments in many states is severely confined, principally by state-imposed rather than locally determined restrictions. There is a need for state studies of these restrictions, which take various legislative and constitutional forms—ceilings on property tax rates and total indebtedness; exemptions from local taxation of state-owned, veterans' and homestead property; and legislative withholding of, or specific prohibition against, authority for local governments to broaden their revenue sources. Studies by the states on other matters that bear directly on local finances are also necessary—for example, the extensiveness and distribution of state grants-in-aid and shared taxes and the methods of tax assessment and tax administration. Moreover, if under revised programs of financing an important part of local revenues is to be state-derived, the states of necessity will have to review such limitations on their own financing ability as are currently stipulated by constitutional and legislative provisions.

Improvements in administrative organization and in administrative methods are essential to strengthen many local governments. The over-

---

[6] There is further need for acceleration of the school district consolidation movement. States may also wish to investigate the merits of consolidating certain counties and merging some independent school districts with general local governments. For various reasons, however, the latter two changes seem less likely to materialize than the other suggestions, which are generally more central to the problem of adequate area.

The Responsibilities of the States

abundance of independently elected policy-making and administrative officials and semi-independent boards constitute small, detached empires immune from effective central direction and control. Organizational arrangements should be simplified and more fully integrated to facilitate better performance and more adequate public accountability. Similarly, the administrative methods of many local governments require modernization. Too many local governments are not using well-recognized and extensively tested practices concerning personnel, finance, planning and purchasing. If counties are to be converted into satisfactory metropolitan units, their shortcomings in organization and methods as well as in financing ability should first be eliminated. In some instances it may be advisable for the states to furnish direct and vigorous leadership to bring renovations in local administrative organizations and to supply supervision and technical and advisory assistance to foster stronger administrative methods.

The granting of home rule as to administrative organization and methods is not inconsistent with the previous recommendation for merging or abolishing various local governments. "It defeats the purpose of home rule," the Commission on Intergovernmental Relations emphasized, "to resist needed consolidation of local units by interpreting home rule as a right of perpetual self-determination. Self-determination in one isolated local unit of a large community restricts the opportunity for genuine home rule in the whole community." Nor is a grant of home rule in conflict with the suggestion that more supervision and technical and advisory assistance by the state government may be necessary. "The statewide enforcement of some degree of uniformity in the common interest," the Commission stated, "may in the long run strengthen, rather than weaken, home rule by ensuring that local action will be more satisfying to the public."[7]

Many local governments are also inadequate because they do not possess sufficient freedom from detailed state legislation in performing their functions. Too much legislation of this type adds to the burdens of state legislatures and diverts them from important state-wide matters. It hampers local governments in their efforts to respond to the community needs of their residents. Granting broader discretion to local governments in the exercise of their powers and establishing flexible administrative supervision, consultation and technical assistance at the

[7] Commission on Intergovernmental Relations, *Report*, pp. 54, 55.

state level are measures that will strengthen both state and local governments and will aid in equipping local units to be effective members of metropolitan organizations.[8]

A Research and Service Agency

The responsibilities of the states in establishing adequate metropolitan units and in appraising and improving local governments are very important but are not in themselves complete answers to the metropolitan problem. The states have a further important responsibility. It is recommended that each state create or adapt an agency to aid in determining the present and changing needs of its metropolitan and nonmetropolitan areas. Activities of the agency should include analysis and recommendation on the effects in such areas of current and contemplated policies of all governments and major private organizations. Such a state agency will serve as a focal point of information and evaluation about metropolitan and local conditions and relations and it will develop both remedial and preventive programs. The importance of agencies of this type is not confined to states that contain metropolitan areas; they can assist in strengthening local governments both in non-metropolitan and metropolitan sections.

Numerous duties are appropriate to such a state agency. It should have continuing responsibility for studying the following matters and recommending on them to the appropriate groups and individuals:

> Legal changes that are necessary for the establishment of adequate metropolitan and local levels of government.
>
> The various methods of adopting a metropolitan form of government.
>
> The voting procedure to be employed if local determination is used as the method of adoption.
>
> The need for subsequent adjustments in area, organization, functions and finance of reorganized governments.
>
> The governmental needs of local areas as significant changes start to emerge—for example, areas that begin to take on metropolitan characteristics.
>
> The nature and extent of the problems of particular areas.
>
> Interstate metropolitan areas that include part of the territory of the state.

[8] For further appraisals of local governmental deficiencies in area, finance, organization, procedure, and discretion in the use of powers, see Commission on Intergovernmental Relations, *Report* (Washington: 1955), pp. 47–55 and Council of State Governments, *State-Local Relations* (Chicago: 1946).

The Responsibilities of the States

> The merits of state advisory and technical services and administrative supervision to governments in local areas.
>
> The effect of present and proposed state government programs, including grants-in-aid, upon local areas.
>
> The impact of existing and contemplated actions of the national government—such as fiscal policies, public utility regulation and civil defense directives—on local areas.
>
> The results of present and planned activities of local governments, such as urban redevelopment and public housing, upon local areas.
>
> The consequences for local areas of current and anticipated decisions of major private organizations on such matters as sites for commercial and industrial activities and locations of terminal and transfer facilities.
>
> The means of facilitating greater coordination of existing and contemplated policies of the national, state and local governments and of private associations and individuals that affect local areas.

In performing these functions, the agency should carry on active and continuous programs of research and service. It should make studies itself or in collaboration with others, on its own initiative as well as at the request of public officials or responsible private groups. When territory of its state is involved in an interstate metropolitan area, it should undertake studies in cooperation with similar agencies in adjoining states or assist interstate commissions that are created specifically for the purpose. It can be of great usefulness in assisting the governor and legislature in their consideration of proposals affecting governments at the metropolitan and local levels.

Necessarily, such an agency will have to be staffed by a sufficient number of professionally trained, experienced and adequately compensated individuals. Although part of its activities will be highly specialized, some of its reports should be specifically designed to give the public a wider knowledge and better understanding of metropolitan and local problems and developments.

At present these matters, basic and extremely important to the welfare of metropolitan and non-metropolitan areas, are receiving inadequate attention. Some of them are not obtaining serious scrutiny at all, and others are subject to temporary or piecemeal analysis at different levels of government. Urgent necessity exists for systematic, interrelated and continuing consideration of all of the enumerated matters through a new or reorganized state agency.

These activities should be carried out by a single agency in each state. But their proper performance does not depend on locating the functions in the same place in all state governments. There are various possibilities.

The duties can be assigned to any one of several agencies:

> A new staff agency closely associated with or in the office of the governor.
>
> An existing department of administration.
>
> An existing department of finance.
>
> An existing planning or planning and development agency that is an independent board or a part of a major department.
>
> A new office of planning services placed in the office of the governor or made co-equal with the budget office in an integrated department of administration or department of finance, organized along the lines suggested in the recent report of the Council of State Governments, *Planning Services for State Government*.
>
> A new state planning office responsible to the governor, created along lines suggested in the National Municipal League's *Model State and Regional Planning Law* of 1954.
>
> An existing agency responsible for financial supervision of local governments.
>
> A professional research staff serving an administrative tribunal or special court, noted earlier in Part Three as a means for putting metropolitan reorganizations into effect.
>
> A new permanent commission composed of public officials or private citizens or both and aided by research analysts.
>
> An existing or new joint legislative interim committee that functions on a continuing basis.

If the responsibilities are allotted to an existing agency, certain guides are pertinent. (1) These highly significant functions should not be made a minor phase of some part of the state government. If they are assigned to a department of administration or finance, for example, or to an office responsible for financial supervision of local units, care should be taken that they are not relegated to an unimportant status because of other responsibilities of the organization. (2) Consideration should be given to whether it is advisable or inadvisable to assign these duties to an agency that currently possesses functions of a supervisory or enforcement nature. (3) The functions involved should not be allocated to organizations currently performing largely dissimilar services without first reorienting these existing activities to make them sufficiently comparable. Some planning and development agencies that concentrate mainly on industrial promotion are illustrations.

Whether the duties—which consist of collecting and appraising data and formulating proposed action programs—are given to a new or existing agency, they should be located close to the principal centers of decision making. Otherwise their effectiveness may be negligible.

A Continuing Responsibility for the States

Metropolitan areas are dynamic, ever changing concentrations of people who live, work and play in the midst of a complex series of governmental and private relationships. The responsibilities of the states for the welfare of these areas are large today in terms of authorizing the establishment of adequate governmental machinery, in providing a focal point of information and analysis about metropolitan conditions and relations, and in supplying assistance, plans and services in particular fields. If the metropolitan trend continues, the population of more states will become largely metropolitan. Increasing interrelationships will develop between nearby metropolitan areas, whether or not state lines are involved. And more interstate areas will emerge. The responsibilities of the states certainly will not lessen under such circumstances. So long as there are metropolitan areas the states, in combination with the interest, support and participation of local units and citizens, seem destined to play strategic roles of much importance to the people of the nation as a whole.

The experience of the United States and other nations demonstrates that public problems change from decade to decade and from generation to generation. Such has been and will continue to be the experience with the metropolitan problem. The metropolitan problem, which is one of growth and development, alters as the factors that affect it fluctuate. What are suitable solutions today may be inadequate ten, twenty or thirty years from now. What is necessary, therefore, is to appraise and act on the metropolitan problem as it currently exists, and then constantly to reappraise and act in the light of future developments. Only in this way can our governmental organizations in metropolitan areas be suitable instruments for satisfying the needs of our people.

INDEX

Alameda County, California, 84, 87–88, 92–95, 104
Albany, New York, 12
Albuquerque, New Mexico, 9, 32
Allegheny County, Pennsylvania, 87–88, 92–95, 104
   Urban county charter, 108–109
Amarillo, Texas, 37
American Bar Association, Section on Municipal Law, 131
American Municipal Association, 130
American Political Science Association, 130–31
Annexation, 25–52, 138
   Administrative agency proposed, 48–49
   Boundary determination, 44–45
   Central cities annexing largest areas, 1948–54 (table), 31
   Courts, 42–43, 137
   Cross-county, 28
   Decade of annexation activity, 1945–54 (table), 30
   Enabling Act, Texas, 36
   Fringe areas, 32–40, 50–51
   Home Rule Amendment, Texas, 36
   Home rule charters, 37–39
   Home rule cities, 35–40
   Judicial determination, 41–49
   Large areas, 25–26, 31, 136, 139
   Legislation, legal procedure, 26–52, 136
      Implementation, 49–52
   Methods used in various states, 34–35
   Proceedings, methods of initiating, 41–42
   Publicity, 50–51
   Rights of decline and appeal, 46
   Selective, 39–40
   Small areas, 29–30
   Terms and conditions, 45–46
   Use, in connection with city-county separation, 82–83, 85
Arapahoe County, Colorado, 80
Ashland, Kentucky, 13
Atlanta, Georgia, 12, 30, 32, 71
   Transfer of county activities to city, 114
Austin, Texas, 37, 71

Bain, Chester W., 48–49, 83
Baltimore, Maryland, 110–11
   City-county separation, 76–81, 85
Baltimore County, Maryland
   Urban county plan, 110–11

Baton Rouge, Louisiana
   City-county consolidation, 53, 65–72, 104, 137
Bay City, Michigan, 14
Bibb County, Georgia, 73
Birmingham, Alabama, 72
Borough plan, see Federation (The borough plan)
Boroughs (New York plan), 63–64
   Coterminous with counties of same name, 63
Boston, Massachusetts, 7, 12, 72, 120
   City-county consolidation, 53, 54–56, 69
   Federation plans, 87, 92–95
Brockton, Massachusetts, 12
Bronx, Borough, New York, 63–65
Brooklyn, New York
   City-county consolidation, 61–62
Brooklyn, Borough, New York, 63–64
Buffalo, New York, 14
   Functional transfers, 107

California, 10, 84, 120, 131
   Functions, transfer of, from cities to counties, 111–13; (table), 112
      Legal authorizations, 111–13
   Growth of urban county development, 111–13
Carondolet, Missouri, 26
Central cities, 3
   Annexing largest areas, 1948–54 (table), 31
Central counties, 3–4
Characteristics of metropolitan areas, 7–8
Charlotte, North Carolina, 71
Charters, see under Annexation; City-county consolidation; Federation (The borough plan); also Home rule charters; Urban charters
Chelsea, Massachusetts, 55–56
Chicago, Illinois, 14, 15, 31, 120, 131
Chicago Transit Authority, 121
Citizen control of metropolitan areas, 21–22
City-county consolidation, 53–75, 104, 139
   Adoption, by over-all vote, 66, 136–37
   Appraisal, 74–75
   Areas involved, 69–71
   Charter, 65
   Court decisions, 58
   Early developments, 69

City-county consolidation (*continued*)
  Educational activities unified in New York City areas, 64–65
  Financial and other arrangements in Boston consolidation, 54–56
  General conclusions, 68–71
  Interlocking governments, 67–68
  Reallocation of functions to city, 70
  Rejected consolidation proposals, 71–74
  State enabling law, 59–60
  State legislative acts, 54, 57–58, 69, 136, 137
  Variations in form, 53
City-county separation, 54, 76–85, 140
  Appraisal, 85
  Area and population of four separated governments, 80; (table), 80
  Boundary changes, effects, 82–83
  Characteristics of Virginia separations, 81–82
  Governmental units, increase in number, 85
  Negligible recent interest, 83–84
  Remainder of county, disposition, 77–78
  State constitutional authorization, 76–77, 85
  State legislation, 77, 85
  Territorial enlargement at time of separation and later, 77–80, 85
  Territorial enlargement through annexation, 82–83, 85
Cleveland, Ohio, 14, 72, 131
  Functional transfers, 107–108
Commission on Intergovernmental Relations, *Report*, 1955, 130
Conference, national, on metropolitan problems, 131
Corpus Christi, Texas, 37
County governmental activities, 53–75
County officials
  Appointed by city government, 60–61
  Appointed by governor, 56
  Independently elected, 54, 56, 58, 63
Cuyahoga County, Ohio, 72, 131
  Functional transfers, 107–108

Dade County, Florida, 72, 73
  Federation plan, 87–88, 92–95; (table), 89–91
  Urban county charter, 109–10
  Urban county plan, 108
Dallas, Texas, 30, 31, 32, 37, 39
Dallas County, Texas, 39
Davidson County, Tennessee, 50
Decentralization of metropolitan areas, 12
Definitions of metropolitan areas, 3–5
Denver, Colorado, 12
  City-county separation, 76–81, 83, 85
Detroit, Michigan, 12, 14
District of Columbia, 13
Duluth, Minnesota, 14
Durham, North Carolina, 71
Duval County, Florida, 73

East Baton Rouge Parish (County), Louisiana, 65–68, 137
Economic Report of the President, 1955, 20, 130
Elizabeth City County, Virginia, 73, 74, 83
Enabling legislation, *see under* Annexation; City-county consolidation; Metropolitan special districts
Erie, Pennsylvania, 14
Erie County, New York
  Functional transfers, 107

Federal Committee on Standard Metropolitan Areas, 3
Federation (The borough plan), 86–104, 133, 135–36
  Adoption by area voters, 95–96
  Appraisal, 103–104
  Attempts at adoption of plan, 86–96
  Charter form, 94–95
  Governmental functions, division, 88, 91–92; (table), 89–91
  Metropolitan governing board, composition, 92–93
  State constitutional authorization, 93–94
  See also Toronto, Canada, federation plan
Financial arrangements
  City-county consolidations, 55–56, 66–67
  City-county separation, 85
  Metropolitan special districts, 120–21
Fort Worth, Texas, 37, 39
Fresno, California, 34, 131
Fringe areas
  Annexation, 32–40, 50–51
  Benefits, 32–33, 38
  Incorporation, 38–39, 49
Fulton County, Georgia
  Transfer of some functions to Atlanta, 114
Functional transfers and joint efforts, 105–16, 140
  Appraisal, 114–15
  Major characteristics, 105–106
  Urban or metropolitan county movement, 106–14

Index

Galveston, Texas, 37
Geographical location of metropolitan areas, by states (table), 7
Georgia, 13
Gilbertson, H. S., 115
Government Affairs Foundation, 130
Governmental activities
   City-county consolidation, 53–75
   Division, under federation plan, 88, 91–92; (table), 89–91
   Service and regulatory defects, 18–19, 33, 38, 40, 44
   See also under Counties; Metropolitan special districts
Governmental complexity of metropolitan areas, 15–17, 129
Governmental organization
   Boroughs, under New York Plan, 63–65
   Interlocking governments, 67–68
   Metropolitan areas, inadequacy, 17–18, 129
   Metropolitan special districts, 120
Governments, local, *see* Local governments
Governors' Conference, 1955, 130
Grand Prairie, Texas, 39

Hampton, Virginia, 83
Harris County, Texas, 131
Hennepin County, Minnesota, 84
Home rule, 143
Home Rule Amendment, Texas, 36
Home rule charters, 37–39, 108, 110–11
Home rule cities
   Annexation, 35–40
   Defensive and competitive races to annex or incorporate, 38–39
Houston, Texas, 30, 31, 32, 37, 39, 71, 131
Huntington, West Virginia, 13

Idaho, 8
Illinois, 13, 120, 131
Incorporation
   Fringe areas, 38–39, 49
   Suburban areas, 38–39
Indiana, 13
Intercounty metropolitan areas, 12–13, 136
Inter-local cooperative agreements, 138
Interstate metropolitan areas, 13–14; (table), 14, 136
Intracounty metropolitan areas, 12–13, 136

Jackson County, Missouri, 72
Jacksonville, Florida, 73
Jefferson County, Alabama, 72
Jefferson County, Kentucky, 72
Jefferson Parish, Louisiana, 54
Joint efforts, *see* Functional transfers and joint efforts

Kansas City, Kansas, 72
Kansas City, Missouri, 51, 72, 139
Kentucky, 13
King County, Washington, 72, 84, 131–32
Kings County, New York, 61–62
Knoxville, Tennessee, 12

Legislation, *see under* Annexation; City-county consolidation; City-county separation; Federation (The borough plan); Metropolitan special districts
Local governmental units of metropolitan areas, 14–15; (table), 16
Local governments, 140–44
   Deficiencies in citizen control, 21–22
   Financial inequalities and weaknesses, 20–21, 142
   Inadequate structure, 17–18, 141
   Service and regulatory defects, 18–19, 33, 38, 40, 44, 141
   Shortcomings, 141–43
Location of metropolitan areas, by states (table), 7
Long Branch, Canada, 98
Los Angeles, California, 9, 84, 120, 139
Los Angeles County, California, 139
Louisiana, 53
Louisiana Territory, 53
Louisville, Kentucky, 50, 72
Lubbock, Texas, 9

Macon, Georgia, 73
Madison, Wisconsin, 15
Manhattan, Borough, New York, 63–65
Massachusetts, 13, 55
Metropolitan county movement, 106–11
Metropolitan governing body
   Composition, under federation plans
      Toronto, 101
      United States, 92–93
Metropolitan special districts, 33, 117–23, 134, 140; by state (table), 124–26
   Enabling laws, 118
   Finance, 120–21
   Governmental organization, 119–20
   Location, 120
Metropolitan units, 133–34
   Authorizing, 132–40
      Principles advisable as guides, 132–33

Metropolitan units (*continued*)
  Methods of adoption, 136–38
Metropolitan Water District of Southern California, 121
Miami, Florida, 9, 72, 73, 87, 108–10
Milwaukee, Wisconsin, 14, 51, 72
  Functional transfers, 107
Milwaukee County, Wisconsin, 72
  Functional transfers, 107
Mimico, Canada, 98
Minneapolis, Minnesota, 12, 30, 84
Minnesota, 84
Missouri, 35
Montana, 8
Multipurpose metropolitan districts, 133–35
Multnomah County, Oregon, 72, 84

Nashville, Tennessee, 50
Nevada, 8
New England, 4
New Jersey, 13
New Mexico, 35
New Orleans, Louisiana, 12
  City-county consolidation, 53–54
New York City, 7, 15, 119, 139
  City-county consolidation, 53, 61–65, 69–71
New York County, New York, 61–65
Newport News, Virginia, 47, 73, 74, 82, 83
Norfolk, Virginia, 47, 50
North Dakota, 8

Oakland, California, 9, 12, 84, 87, 119, 120
Ohio, 13, 35, 120, 131
Oklahoma City, Oklahoma, 51
Ontario (Province), Canada, 35, 137
Oregon, 84, 131

Parish of Orleans, Louisiana, 53, 54
Pennsylvania, 10, 13
Philadelphia, Pennsylvania, 7, 15, 119
  City-county consolidation, 53, 57–61, 69–71
Philadelphia County, Pennsylvania, 57–61
Phoebus, Virginia, 83
Phoenix, Arizona, 9
Pittsburgh, Pennsylvania, 12, 31, 87, 108–109
Population
  Estimated civilian population, by metropolitan areas and non-metropolitan territory: April, 1955 (table), 11
  Metropolitan areas, 3–5, 8–11, 129
  Non-metropolitan, 11
Suburban, 9–10
Trends, 10–12, 129
Portland, Oregon, 72, 84
Portsmouth, Virginia, 47
Public improvements, 45–46

Queens, Borough, New York, 63–64
Queens County, New York, 62

Ramsey County, Minnesota, 72
Recommendations on the metropolitan problem
  Suggested program for the states, 128
  Various organizations, 132
Research and service agencies, state, 144–46
  Duties, 144–45
  Guides to be followed, 146
Revere, Massachusetts, 55
Richmond, Borough, New York, 63–64
Richmond, Virginia, 47
Richmond County, New York, 62
Roanoke, Virginia, 47

Sacramento, California, 51, 131
St. Louis, Missouri, 26, 119, 131
  City-county consolidation, 73, 74, 104, 137
  City-county separation, 76–81, 85
  Federation plan, 87–88, 93–95
St. Louis County, Missouri, 26, 73, 78, 87–88, 93–95, 104
  Urban county plan, 110
St. Paul, Minnesota, 12, 72
Salt Lake City, Utah, 84
San Antonio, Texas, 30, 31, 32, 37, 39, 51, 71
San Diego, California, 9, 84
San Francisco, California, 9, 12, 119
  City-county separation, 76–81, 85
  Federation plan, 87–88, 92–96, 104
San Jose, California, 51
San Mateo County, California, 78, 79, 87–88, 92–96, 104
Schenectady, New York, 12
School districts, 54, 57
Seattle, Washington, 72, 84, 131
Special districts, *see* Metropolitan special districts
States
  Responsibilities, 129–47
  Suggested program, 128
Studies of the metropolitan problem, by various groups, 131–32

Index

Suburban areas
  Incorporation, 38–39
  Population, 9–10
  Urban county plan, 110–11
Suburbanization, 27
Suffolk County, Massachusetts, 54–56
Superior, Minnesota, 14

Territorial limits and growth of metropolitan areas, 3–6, 129
Texas
  Annexation, 35–40
  City-county consolidation, 73
  Home rule cities, 35–40
Toledo, Ohio, 14, 71, 120
Toronto, Canada
  Federation plan, 96–103, 138
  Governmental functions of metropolitan area, distribution, 99–100
  Reorganization of metropolitan area, 96–98
Towns, 4
Troy, New York, 12

Urban county areas, 133, 136
Urban county charters, 108–11
Urban county movement, 106–11
Utah, 131

Vermont, 8
Virginia
  Annexation, 35, 40–49, 82, 137
  City-county separation, 76, 81–83, 85

Warwick County, Virginia, 73, 74, 83
Washington, D.C., 9, 13–14
Washington, State, 84
  City-county consolidation, 73
Wichita Falls, Texas, 37
Winthrop, Massachusetts, 55
Wisconsin, 131
Wyandotte County, Kansas, 72
Wyoming, 8

York County, Canada, 97